SECRETS OF
WARFARE

SECRETS OF WARFARE

EXPOSING THE MYTHS AND HIDDEN HISTORY OF WEAPONS AND BATTLES

WILLIAM WEIR

Author of *50 Battles That Changed the World*

New Page Books
A division of The Career Press, Inc.
Pompton Plains, N.J.

SECRETS OF WARFARE
EDITED AND TYPESET BY KARA KUMPEL
Cover design by Joseph Sherman/Dutton and Sherman
Printed in the U.S.A.
Images on pages 19, 32, 55, 68, 108, and 120 are taken from the Library of Congress.
Images on pages 23, 28, 36, 51, 62, 63, and 131 © *Weapons and Armor: A Pictorial Archive of Woodcuts and
Engravings*.
Images on pages 92 and 112 are taken from iStock photo.
Images on page 102, 145, 160, 164, 171, 174, 176, 190, 218, and 222 are taken from the National Archives.
Images on pages 134 and 152 are courtesy of William Weir.
Image on page 210 is courtesy of the U.S. Army.

To order this title, please call toll-free 1-800-CAREER-1 (NJ and Canada:
201-848-0310) to order using VISA or MasterCard, or for further information on books from Career Press.

The Career Press, Inc.
220 West Parkway, Unit 12
Pompton Plains, NJ 07444
www.careerpress.com
www.newpagebooks.com

Library of Congress Cataloging-in-Publication Data
Weir, William, 1928-
    Warfare: exposing the myths and hidden history of weapons and battles / by William Weir.
        p. cm.
    Includes bibliographical references and index.
    ISBN 978-1-60163-155-8 -- ISBN 978-1-60163-671-3 (ebook)
        1. Military history--Anecdotes. 2. Military art and science--History--Anecdotes.
    3. Battles--History--Anecdotes. I. Title.
D25.5.W43 2011
355.02--dc22
                                                                    2011010737

For William,
from Grandpa

Acknowledgments

As I am not old enough to have talked with Thucydides or Henry V (although it sometimes feels as if I am), I have had to rely on many, many authors, from Xenophon to John Keegan. All of these sources are greatly appreciated; you will find their names in the Bibliography.

Two modern authorities not included in the list of books have also been most helpful. One is my friend and neighbor, John White of Cheshire, Connecticut, who as a Naval officer during the Vietnam War, was one of the first to question whether the alleged second attack on U.S. ships in the Tonkin Gulf ever occurred.

Another is the late Joseph E. Smith of the Army Materiel Command, who explained why the Philippine Moros, although they played a very small part in the Philippine War, are often mentioned as our only enemies in that conflict. (Briefly: The Moros were terrifying. Smith's father was a soldier in Moroland after the main war was over. In those days, individual Moros would often take an oath to die killing unbelievers. Fueled by religious fanaticism and drugs, the Filipino Muslims were hard to stop. The elder Smith saw a Moro *juramentado* [Spanish for "one who has taken an oath"] kill several American and Filipino Christians even though he had been hit 30 times by buckshot from a 12-gauge shotgun, a .45-70 caliber rifle, and a .30-06 caliber rifle.)

Contents

Introduction

There are some things that most of us reasonably well-read people have known almost all our lives. We know, for example, that the *Monitor* and the *Virginia* (formerly the *Merrimack*) were not the first ironclad ships built. The first was French, and the second was British.

We think we know these things, but we don't.

The first battle between ironclads was fought in 1592, and it was fought in Korean, not American waters. And it involved two of history's most remarkable leaders, a Korean and a Japanese.

We've heard of the "cavalry cycle" that began when mounted Gothic lancers annihilated a Roman army back in AD 378. From then until the late 14th and early 15th centuries, when English archers shot three armies of French knights to pieces, we've been told, the armored knight ruled the battlefield.

We haven't been told how lowly infantrymen turned William the Bastard into William the Conqueror in 1066, nor, for that matter, how the French managed to win the Hundred Years' War, although the English—not they—had the longbow.

But not all military myths concern events in the dim, dark, ancient and medieval past. Some would have us believe that only a third of the American colonists favored independence, while a third favored the monarchy and another third was neutral. They don't explain why, with few exceptions, *all* the militia favored independence, nor what motivated the relatively few Tories on the other side. It wasn't affection for King George.

Fast-forward to times many of us today can remember. Today, many Americans are convinced that General Douglas MacArthur was the greatest American military hero of the 20th century. But many (like the author) who served in the Korean War are not convinced. Veterans of the Vietnam War are also unconvinced of many strongly held beliefs about their war.

In the early years of World War II, we heard about the power of the German tanks and how the Allies had no armor to compare with them. And we know that the two nuclear bomb raids on Hiroshima and Nagasaki were the most deadly in history. That's not true either.

In many cases, the truth really is stranger than fiction. For example, what could be stranger than the mysterious high-speed dirigible that a respected New Jersey physician invented during the Civil War? But even stranger is the fact that the government rejected it while Confederate troops were sitting in Washington's suburbs.

In military "history" there are oodles of myths. Here are some of them, along with the truth and, where known, the motives of the myth-makers.

MYTH #1

Western Military Superiority Dates From Ancient Times

Geoffrey Parker, editor of the *Cambridge Illustrated History of Warfare*, is one of the most prominent proponents of this myth. He lists a number of Western military traditions that led to European domination of the world. These include superior technology and discipline, with discipline being the more important. "A technology edge, however, has rarely been sufficient in itself to ensure victory," he says.[1] Ruthlessness is another important factor in the rise of the West, according to Parker. "The overall aim of Western strategy, whether by battle, siege or attrition, almost always remained the total defeat and destruction of the enemy, and this contrasted sharply with the military practice of many other societies."[2] Parker contrasts the aims of the New England colonists with those of the Narragansetts, who strongly disapproved of the way the colonists fought: "'It was too furious,' one brave told an English captain in 1638, 'and it slays too many men.' The captain did not deny it: the Indians, he speculated, 'might fight seven years and not kill seven men.'"[3]

And it's true. The New England colonists were far more ruthless than their Native American neighbors. (They were also more ruthless than their fellow Europeans from Spain. Compare the percentage of the U.S. population who have Native American blood with that of Mexico.) To the "Indians" of North America, war was an opportunity to demonstrate their bravery. A man got far more honor for touching an enemy with his hand than for shooting him with a bow or a gun. Native Americans in the technologically more advanced societies in what is now Latin America fought to obtain captives to sacrifice to their gods rather than to annihilate their enemies.

But most non-European societies were not Native Americans. When it comes to ruthlessness, few Europeans could hold a candle to Genghis Khan or Tamerlane. And did Europeans usually triumph over more numerous non-European enemies when both sides had roughly equal technology? Take Marathon: although the opponents were not technologically equal, the Persians were not hopelessly outclassed. In restricted space, like the Plain of Marathon, the Greek phalanx, a moving wall of bronze pushing a mass of spears, was far superior to anything the lightly armed Persians could field. Greek numbers may have been superior, too. There were 10,000 Athenians and 1,000 Plateans, according to Herodotus. Herodotus doesn't say how many Persians there were, but he says they came in 600 ships. Those ships carried rowers, who didn't normally fight on land, and they also carried horses. Admiral W.L. Rodgers, a student of galley warfare, estimates there could have been as many as 15,000 Persians or as few as 4,000.[4]

The Battle of Marathon, an important but hardly decisive battle.

But the Persians didn't plan to wipe out the Athenian army on the Plain of Marathon. They were carrying out a plan hatched by Darius the Great, a leader with far more talent than he is usually given credit for. Darius was a usurper, not the legitimate heir of Cyrus the Great and his son, Cambyses. He had managed to take the Persian throne, restore Cyrus's crumbling empire, and organize a competent administration. He was not, like Cyrus, a great general, but he was a competent one. He was not, again like Cyrus, a humanitarian. Cyrus promised his people freedom of religion, abolished slavery, and returned captive populations, like the Jews, to their homelands.[5] Darius didn't liberate anyone, and he allowed slavery, though not to the extent that existed in Greece. But Darius was a statesman and a politician, a man who knew how to get his way without excessive bloodshed.

The trouble had begun when the Ionian Greek cities in Asia Minor revolted against Persian rule. Those cities had been led by tyrants, leaders without the royal blood Greeks of that time expected of their kings. Darius had crushed the revolt and deposed the tyrants. He set up pseudo-democracies: the Greek citizens could make their own laws, but they had to be approved by the Great King. The Greek commander at the Battle of Marathon, Miltiades, had been one of those displaced tyrants.

During the Ionian Revolt, Athens and Eretria had aided the Ionians. Now Darius was getting his revenge. He had no intention of overwhelming Greece with a huge army and navy. Greece, rocky, mountainous land, could not support a large army: supplies would have to come by sea. Greek naval power was formidable, and the Aegean was a stormy sea with rocky shores. Instead of force, Darius would use guile. He cultivated fifth columns in Athens and Eretria and promised to liberate citizens from their upper-class oppressors. The traitors would open the gates of their cities and let in the Persian troops. So the Persian monarch sent a small force across the sea, first to Eretria, then to Athens. The Persian troops would distract the Eretrian and Athenian armies so the traitors could open their cities' gates.

Darius made only one mistake. He put the force under a Median general named Datis. Datis was probably a good battlefield commander—he had to be, because he held high command even though he was not an ethnic Persian. But he was a conservative old soldier. When the people of Eretria opened their gates, Datis rounded them all up and made them slaves. That's the way it had always been done.

Datis's action put a crimp in his master's plan for taking over Athens. Persian agents were persuasive, though, and

Persian gold flowed freely. Miltiades, standing in the hills above Marathon with his troops, a position they had taken to neutralize the Persian cavalry, saw a flash of sunlight from distant Athens, probably a reflection from a polished shield. Then he saw the Persians loading their ships.

Miltiades knew the situation was desperate. Traveling by sea, the Persian army could get to Athens before the Athenian troops. Miltiades ordered the troops to fall in. There were 10 divisions, each with its own general. The generals rotated command. Today was Miltiades' day. Normally, the Greek phalanx was eight ranks deep. To lengthen his line and give the Persian cavalry no room for flanking moves, Miltiades made the center of his line only four ranks deep. Flanking units would be eight ranks deep.

The Greek army marched down the hillsides, a clanking bronze glacier bristling with spears, the men marching in step to the music of flutes. The Persian archer began shooting when the Greeks were 200 yards away, but their arrows wouldn't penetrate Greek armor. The bronze glacier changed to an avalanche as the Greeks switched to double time.

The center of the Persian line was held by ethnic Persians and Sakas, a Scythian people. They fought fiercely, even trying to climb the bronze wall of shields while thrusting with daggers and chopping with axes. The Greek center bent back while the stronger ends of the line pushed forward against the somewhat unenthusiastic troops of Persia's subject nations. It looked like the beginning of Cannae, Hannibal's masterpiece of more than two centuries later. But Miltiades could not, like Hannibal, complete the encirclement of his enemies. The Persians ran for their ships. The Greeks followed, but they captured only seven of the 600 ships. The bulk of the Persian army got away.

The Greeks had won, but the situation was still grave. The Persians would get to Athens before the Athenian army. Miltiades summoned Pheidippides, a professional runner, and told him to go back to Athens and tell citizens that their army had defeated the Persians.

Pheidippides ran his heart out—literally. He dashed into Athens crying "Nike! Nike!" ("Victory! Victory!") and dropped dead. When the Persian fleet arrived, Darius's troops found the gates closed and barred. The gates stayed closed until the victorious Greek army returned.

So ended what is universally acknowledged to be one of the most decisive battles of the world. There were no rivers of blood or mountains of corpses. There was heroism: Pheidippides, for one example, and the unarmored Persians and Sakas who attacked the Greek phalanx with daggers, for another. But there was no fight to the death against overwhelming odds. It was not a case of a Western David defeating an Eastern Goliath.

The Persians may have had more men than the Greeks, or they may have had fewer. But there was no question who had the larger force when, three and a half centuries later, the Romans invaded what had been Persia, now called Parthia.

Marcus Licinius Crassus, one third of the triumvirate who ruled Rome, was leading 40,000 infantry and 4,000 cavalry across the Parthian desert. Crassus planned to defeat the Parthians, take over their empire, and continue on to India and perhaps China. It shouldn't be too hard—the Parthians had been desert nomads, mere barbarians, a few generations ago. They were nowhere near as powerful as the ancient Persians, who had been conquered by Alexander. And weren't Romans better men than Macedonians and Greeks?

The Romans were engaging in a seemingly endless pursuit of Parthian light cavalry when an Arab who had previously given the Romans valuable information appeared. He told Crassus he knew a shortcut to the Parthian army, which was much smaller than the Roman. Crassus took the shortcut, which was over waterless wasteland, and he did meet the Parthians.

He met them suddenly.

The Parthian general, king of the subordinate kingdom of Suren, was known to the Romans as Surena. He was a young man, only 30, but he had a reputation for both wisdom and courage. He would need both, because he had only 10,000 cavalry: 1,000 lancers wearing heavy armor and 9,000 lightly armed horse archers (archers mounted on horses).

Asian horse archers, like these Turks, ruled the steppe for centuries. They destroyed a Roman army at Carrhae and defeated Western armies until the invention of gunpowder.

Surena had hidden his men behind sand dunes, their armor covered with leather so there would be no reflected sunlight to give away their position.

Crassus knew the battle had begun when he heard the thunder of hundreds of horse-mounted kettle drums and the Parthian cavalry appeared on the crests of the dunes. The Parthian heavy cavalry, covered with narrow sheets of steel laced together (called lamelar armor) charged with leveled lances. The Parthian heavy cavalry also carried bows and arrows as secondary weapons. Behind the heavy horsemen came the light horse archers holding their bows.

Roman legionaries had no fear of cavalry. They stood firm and pointed their spears at the horsemen. The Parthians turned away, galloping in all directions. Then the Romans realized that the Parthians had completely surrounded them and were shooting arrows at them from all sides. The Parthians were using an ancient weapon of the Central Asian nomads, the composite bow. This short, extremely flexible bow was composed of layers of sinew, wood, and horn. It was far more sophisticated and powerful than the famous English longbow. It could penetrate Roman armor and outrange any hand weapon in the Roman army. The Parthians were not going to run out of arrows. Surena had brought along a thousand camels loaded with arrows.

Crassus told his son, Publius, to counterattack. Publius had served with Julius Caesar in Gaul and had recruited 1,300 Gaulish horsemen, the best cavalry in the West. He took them, 500 archers, and 4,000 legionaries, and charged. The Parthians fled while shooting over the backs of their horses—what became known as the "Parthian shot." When Publius and his troops were too far from the main body to get help, the Parthian lancers charged. Publius fell back to a defensive position and mighty Roman infantry again stopped the lancers.

Then the Parthian horse archers took over. They surrounded the Romans and shot them all down. The Parthians were using tactics later revived when muskets and cannons replaced spears and bows: If infantry stood firm, they could defeat a cavalry charge with their bayonets, but they then made a wonderful target for the enemy artillery. If they broke ranks and tried to take cover, they foiled the artillery but were vulnerable to the cavalry. The Parthians wiped out Publius's detachment and cut off its leader's head. They threw the head at the Roman main body, which was wilting under the rain of arrows.

Roman survivors tried to escape when darkness fell, but they became scattered. Parthian scouts found Crassus and the group he was leading. They told him that Surena wanted to talk to him about surrender. While Crassus was discussing terms with Surena, a fight broke out between Roman and Parthian troops. Crassus was killed and the remaining Romans enslaved.

According to Parker, utter ruthlessness "became the standard technique for Europeans fighting abroad" from the time of the Greek hoplites (citizen-soldier spearmen) and the Roman legionaries, and this made the Europeans militarily dominant.[6] "Armies from Asia and Africa rarely marched into Europe," he writes, "many of these exceptions—Xerxes, Hannibal, Attila, the Arabs and the Turks—achieved only short-term success."[7] But in fact, the Turks came to Europe in the 15th century and are still there. The Arabs controlled all or part of Spain for twice as long as the British controlled India, and their control was much stricter. The Mongols and Turkish khans controlled Russia—a very big part of Europe—from the 13th to the 16th century. In the 13th century, three divisions of Genghis Khan's army—about 30,000 men—led by Subotai Bahadur and Chepé Noyon, made a reconnaissance in force into Europe. They wiped out the armies of Georgia, Russia, Poland, and

Hungary, and then returned to the Gobi to participate in a council to elect a new Kha-Khan.

The myth of Western superiority sounds as if it was invented to make the reader feel good, to think, "We Westerners are made of sterner stuff than those lesser breeds." At the Battle of Carrhae in 53 BC, the Westerners, ruthless or not, showed no superiority. As a matter of fact, from the time of Carrhae until they could oppose composite bows with practical guns, Europeans were *almost always* defeated by Asian horse archers.

So when you read statements like this: "Once again, the crucial advantage [for Europeans] lay in the ability to compensate for numerical inferiority, for whether defending Europe from invasion (as at Plataea in 476 BC, at Lechfeld in AD 955 and at Vienna in AD 1683) or in subduing Aztec, Inca and Mughal empires, the Western forces have always been outnumbered by at least two to one and often by far more."[8]

...it's time to remember what 10,000 Parthians did to 44,000 Romans, and who won the Crusades. Clear Western military superiority did not exist until the invention of gunpowder.

MYTH #2

The Ancient Greeks Refused to Use Poisoned Arrows

Even though the English words *toxin* and *toxic* come from the Greek word *toxicon*, which itself comes from the Greek *toxon*, meaning "arrow," many "authorities" have long maintained that the ancient Greeks *did not use* poisoned arrows. The Greeks themselves, at the time of the Persian Wars, maintained that arrows were for hunting, not war. Archery was a coward's way of fighting, they believed, and poison was despicable.

In Greek myth, however, there is much written about archery. Odysseus used a bow, although he seems to have left it at home when he went off to the Trojan War, using it only to wipe out his wife's suitors when he finally got back to Ithaca. Herakles was also a famous archer, and he poisoned his arrows with the blood of the Hydra. And how, without recourse to poison, did Paris manage to kill Achilles with an arrow in his *heel*? (Paris, of course *was* a coward, according to both his brother, Hector, and his lover, Helen. But how brave was Achilles, who could dash into battle knowing that the only vulnerable spot on his body was one heel?)

Greek hoplite armed with a mace. Hoplites, who fought in a phalanx, were the world's best heavy infantry for centuries.

Nevertheless, writers in the 19th and early 20th centuries managed to ignore both etymology and these hints from folklore. The people of Western Europe and the United States have long had an idealized view of ancient Greece. At one time, most educated people had studied Greek in school; Greece was the inventor of democracy (a Greek word); pseudo-Greek architecture was the preferred style for public buildings; Greek art was pure, pristine, and unemotional—scholars long refused to believe that the classical Greeks painted their statues. The use of poisoned arrows seemed far too barbaric for these people, especially because in so many of their writings the classical Greeks distained archery. The only way a man should fight, according to those Greeks, was in a hoplite phalanx head to head with his opponent, thrusting with his spear.

Many centuries separated the classical Greeks from their Mycenaean ancestors, whose deeds are recorded in the Iliad, the Odyssey, and all the other myths. Throughout those centuries, details of the old stories changed to make them understandable to the poets' contemporaries. The Mycenaeans used chariots for war, whereas the classical Greeks only used them for sport. Clay tablets found in the ruins of Mycenaean Pylos show large numbers of chariot bodies and chariot wheels stored in royal arsenals. They also show that the kingdom had huge numbers of arrowheads.[1] The ideal weapon to use from a chariot is, of course, the bow and arrow. And the most effective arrows have poisoned tips.

By the mid-20th century, archaeology began to shed new light on Greek archery. Hundreds of arrowheads have been found at Minoan sites on Crete, and hundreds more in the shaft graves of Mycenaean Greece. The Greek arrowheads were made of bronze, flint, and obsidian (volcanic glass). According to A.M. Snodgrass, an authority on ancient Greek weaponry, "Flint is scarce in Greece and it has been suggested that these arrowheads were imported from Egypt; even for obsidian the Mycenaeans had to go as far as Melos in the Cyclades. All this argues an interest in archery perhaps too intensive to be explained in terms of sport or food-gathering."[2]

Incidentally, flint and obsidian can be made far sharper than any metal available in the Bronze Age. They can even be made sharper than steel. A modern archer, Dr. Saxton Pope, experimented with arrows tipped with sharpened steel and with obsidian. In his book, *Bows and Arrows*, he reports, "The most striking phenomenon is the great superiority of the obsidian point in cutting animal tissue."[3]

Unfortunately, archaeology is not able to provide much evidence for the use of poison—a couple of thousand years will obliterate just about any organic substance. However, myths and other writing provide plenty of evidence for the use of poisons, and Adrienne Mayor fills her book, *Greek Fire, Poison Arrows and Scorpion Bombs*, with that evidence.

For example, there's Philotetes, the second-best archer (after Odysseus) in the Greek army that set out for Troy. He had inherited Herakles' poisoned arrows, and accidentally cut himself with one of them. The result was a wound that continually discharged an evil-smelling black ooze. His shipmates could not stand the smell of his wound nor his howls of pain, so they put him ashore on an uninhabited island, Chryse. Philotetes did not starve, though; he survived by shooting birds with his arrows. Apparently the poison, similar to some used today by primitive tribes, caused no harm if eaten. After the Trojan War, the Greeks built a shrine to Philotetes, who had come to be considered a demigod. The shrine contained his bow, his armor, and a bronze image of a snake, a descendant of the fabulous Hydra (and probably the real source of the toxicon a Mycenaean Greek put on his toxon).

MYTH #3

Cavalry Ruled the Battlefield in the Middle Ages

In the year 370, the Huns, a nomadic people originally from the Gobi, attacked the Ostrogoths, or East Goths, a Germanic people originally from Scandinavia, in what is now Russia. The Huns who now appeared in Europe had been driven over the T'ien Shan Mountains by the Chinese centuries ago. They were so far out of sight of the people on the other side of the mountains that a contemporary Hunnish group to the *east* of them was known as the White Huns ("white" being the color of the west in the symbolism of the Far East).[1]

The Huns had moved from their home pastures around the Caspian Sea and the Sea of Aral because other tribes were encroaching on their lands. Life for steppe-dwellers was a game of musical chairs: When drought forced a strong tribe to move, it moved against a weaker nation, which then tried to take over the pastures of a third tribe. The Huns, a conglomeration of independent clans, could not resist the invaders, so

The Huns, here fighting the Goths, ruled an empire
that stretched from Central Asia to Western Europe, and
terrified Western warriors until the death of Attila.

they moved on. Defeat caused the Hunnish clans to unify, and
they developed a powerful military machine.

The basis of the Hunnish machine was weapons and tactics
that had been developing for a thousand years. The main weapon was the composite bow, an improvement of the weapon that
Surenas's Parthians had used to wipe out Crassus's Romans.
On the Eurasian Steppes, all of the clans had organized their

fighting men by tens—10 warriors made a squad, 10 squads made a company, 10 companies (1,000 men) made a battalion, and 10 battalions made a division (the 10,000-man unit the later Mongols called a *tuman*). Under Genghis Khan, these units maneuvered as directed by the waving of a standard. It is not known what, if any, means Attila had of communicating orders, but Hunnish tactics, like Hunnish weapons, were traditional on the steppes: surrounding the enemy and shooting at them from all directions, plus feigned flight to draw the enemy into an ambush or simply to leave them strung out and vulnerable to a mass attack.

The first people the Huns encountered on their march west were the Alans, Iranian nomads the Romans considered the world's most formidable warriors. The Alans had all the weapons and tactics of the Huns and something more—armored lancers. Like the Huns, all the Alanic horsemen had stirrups, a device that would not get to Western Europe for centuries, although the eastern German tribes like the Ostrogoths and the Visigoths also had stirrups. Stirrups let the lancer combine his own weight with that of the horse, so that his lance point struck the enemy with terrible momentum.

What the Alans did not have, though, was unity. Hunnish unity proved to be a more potent factor than Alanic lances. Many of the Alans ended up as part of the Hunnish horde. Others moved west and joined the Ostrogoths. Still other Alanic clans moved into Western Europe. During this period, which saw the breakup of the Western Roman Empire, Alans fought in virtually every war and on both sides of each.

Alans played a prominent part in the next war, the Hunnish attack on the Ostrogoths. Saphrax, one of the two regents of the Ostrogoths after the death of their king, Vithimir, was an Alan.[2] At the same time, Alans made up the vanguard of the Hunnish army.

The Huns' defeat of such powerful nations as the Alans and the Ostrogoths terrified all of non-Roman Europe. Both the Visigoths and the remnants of the Ostrogoths begged the Romans to let them settle in the Empire. The Romans eventually consented, but Roman officials so mistreated the refugees that they revolted.

The Roman emperor, Valens, led the counterattack against the Ostrogoths. He located the Ostrogothic camp, a ring of wagons, similar to the mobile forts of pioneers in the western United States, near the town of Adrianople. The Goths asked to begin negotiations that could lead to peace. Valens sent an envoy to the Gothic camp. The envoy had an escort of undisciplined Spanish archers who opened fire on the wagons as they approached. The Goths behind the wagons replied with an overwhelming barrage of arrows, and the archers fled.

Just then, the regents, Alatheus and Saphrax, emerged from the woods leading a force of Alanic lancers. The nomad horsemen struck the cavalry on the Roman right flank and drove it from the field. The Roman left flank cavalry had hit the wall of wagons but were unable to break through. The Alans and other Ostrogothic cavalry struck the disorganized Roman horses and drove off the rest of the Roman cavalry. Then the "barbarians" turned to the Roman infantry, which was still forming up. The Gothic cavalry hit the Roman infantry from both sides and crowded them so tightly they couldn't draw their swords or throw their spears. Then the mass of the Gothic infantry left their wagon fort and fell on the Romans. The Emperor was killed, and the Romans suffered their worst defeat since the Battle of Cannae in 216 BC.

This battle has been cited as a turning point in warfare, showing the superiority of armored, mounted lancers over infantry, and the beginning of the "cavalry cycle," a time when armored knights dominated all fighting on land. More recently, it has been declared no such thing, because, as T.S. Burns argued, most of the fighting was done by infantry, and the armored knight did not emerge for several centuries.[3] Burns's argument, however, is also a bit shaky. The Alanic and Gothic cavalry certainly set up the Roman defeat, and if the two regents had not appeared when they did, the Romans might well have carried the day. The Medieval knight did not appear for some time, because the Medieval world had not yet appeared. Armored lancers certainly had appeared though, and they had done so many years earlier. The Romans met them when they fought the Persians and Parthians, and they copied these eastern cataphracts (a form of armored heavy cavalry) in their own cavalry.

Still, the idea that Adrianople was a major turning point is as shaky as the idea that there ever was a genuine "cavalry cycle." In 732, more than three and a half centuries after Adrianople, Charles Martel defeated the Muslim cavalry of Abd er-Rahman at Tours with an infantry army. The battle followed an exhausting chase by the Franks after the more mobile Muslims. That led the Franks to add more cavalry to their military.

Still later, in 1066, after knights in all continental European countries had become the military elite, Duke William's knights were repulsed by the English infantry. It took his infantry archers to break the deadlock. They aimed their arrows high into the air so they would fall on the English lines. When the English raised their shields, the Norman lancers charged. The English king, Harold Godwinsson, didn't raise his shield fast enough. He was hit in the eye and knocked out of the fight. A Norman knight later finished him off.

Besiegers pound a castle gate with a battering ram. Cavalry were of litle use in sieges.

Armored knights were effective against raiders like the Vikings, because unless the sea raiders stole horses for land travel (something they frequently did) the knights were much more mobile and able to surprise the Vikings before they could assume a defensive formation. But if spear-armed infantry can form a phalanx, horsemen cannot break through it. Few horses, in fact, could even be induced to try. It took Europe's infantry a few centuries to realize that, but after the Swiss and the Spanish fielded their phalanxes, the day of the decisive cavalry charge was over. Using the phalanx seems like a simple idea, but the last thing the European aristocracy wanted was trained infantry who could defy them.

Missile weapons like the English longbow were another answer to cavalry—as long as the bowmen, like the English archers, were able to hide behind sharpened stakes in the ground.

Furthermore, all throughout the "cavalry cycle" most warfare was siege warfare, and horses are absolutely useless for assaulting stone walls.

Horsemen have always looked down on pedestrians, especially if, like medieval knights, they outranked them socially. But during the Middle Ages, infanty did most of the fighting, although medieval storytellers preferred to give the glory to the mounted knights. After all, it was these mounted nobles who invited the bards to entertain their guests.

Myth #4

Plate Armor Was Enormously Heavy

This myth was reinforced by the movie version of Shakespeare's *Henry V*, which showed the French knights being hoisted into their saddles. In fact, plate armor was less cumbersome than its predecessor, mail. Mail, a kind of fabric made of thousands of iron rings, hung on its wearer like an enormously heavy coat. When a knight lifted his arm, he was also lifting the whole coat. But with plate armor, the only weight he had to contend with was that of his weapon and the plates on his arm.

Plate armor had another advantage over mail: To fight mail-clad knights, the archer or his armorers devised a new kind of arrow point. The old point, the "broadhead," had two cutting edges making a relatively wide triangle. It was designed to cut a path of destruction through blood vessels and muscle to bring down game more quickly. The new point, called a "bodkin," was something like a thick, hardened steel needle. It would enter a link of mail and expand it enough to let the arrow pass through. At close range, a bodkin-equipped arrow would penetrate plate armor, but the range had to be very close. The English archers did most of their damage by wounding and killing the French horses. Thus they were able to turn a charge into chaos.

Suits of plate intended for combat weighed only about 60 pounds—about the same weight as a modern soldier's back-pack, but less constricting because it was distributed over the whole body. The curator of arms and armor at New York's Metropolitan Museum of Art once donned a suit of plate and proceeded to run, jump, and dance in it.

In the late Middle Ages, armor intended solely for "tilting" (jousting on war horses with lances) was often considerably heavier than war armor, and the lances were often designed to be breakable: a broken lance was evidence of a solid hit.[1] Tilting was, after all, a game, albeit a very rough one.

At the Battles of Crecy and Poitiers, most of the English knights fought dismounted, which would have been impos-sible if their plate armor was as heavy as legend has it. The French aristocracy, reluctant to credit the English peasant ar-chers for their defeat, believed that the English won because their knights fought as infantry. So the next time they met, at Agincourt, most of the French knights left their horses be-hind. The field was covered with deep mud, and the enemy was a bit more than half a mile away. Plate armor was good for many things, but slopping through heavy mud was not one of them—particularly for the French nobility, people who never walked anywhere when they could ride. Now the English archers couldn't cause death and confusion by shooting the French horses, but by the time the French dismounted cavalry reached the English line, they were exhausted. English archers were able to knock them down and then kill them with the mauls they used for pounding in the wooden stakes they had set up to stop a cavalry charge.[2]

The idea that armor in the 14th and 15th centuries had become so heavy may have originated as a way to impress others with the power of the English longbow—an important weapon, but one greatly overrated in English-speaking countries.

Later, when muskets replaced bows as the infantry's missile weapons, armor did become uncomfortably heavy. Armorers learned to make breast plates and back plates for both riders and infantry pikemen that most bullets could only dent—even today's bullets. Several years ago the National Rifle Association tested some antique armor pieces by shooting at them with modern pistols and revolvers. Almost all of the bullets bounced off the old breast plates. But by the time that that sort of armor was in style, warfare had changed in a way that made heavy armor more of a handicap than an advantage.

In the Middle Ages, much of the fighting was done by siege: One side stayed in a castle or fortified town, while the other camped outside and attempted to break down the walls or climb over them. There were few long marches. Even when battles took place in open fields, the armies met almost by appointment to slug it out. Hastings, where Harold Godwinsson had to rush down from Stamford Bridge to meet William the Conqueror's army, was an exception. The armor at Hastings was primitive, and the battle itself was more of a Dark Ages than a Middle Ages event.

Myth #5

The English Longbow Was a Phenomenal Weapon

The English had an expression, "drawing the longbow," which meant the same thing as "throwing the bull" in the United States—to exaggerate. It probably originated with people who heard the tall tales from medieval soldiers about what they had done or seen done with the English national weapon. Some of those tales worked their way into folklore and literature, such as the stories of Robin Hood deliberately splitting an arrow already lodged in the center of a target's bull's eye, or how he and his merry men distained regular targets and practiced their marksmanship by shooting at peeled wands, or sticks stripped of their bark.

Not all of the stories concerned the skill of the archers; even more were about the power of the bow. According to most stories, the longbow could send an arrow at least a quarter of a mile with deadly accuracy. A half-mile range was cited more often. And at that range it could penetrate any armor. It greatly outclassed the pitiful crossbows wielded by England's continental enemies and the short bows used by everyone before the introduction of the longbow. The longbow got its power, we are told, because it was so long—equal to the height of the archer.

Now all of this babble was not merely "drawing the long-bow." As the French and the Scots could testify, the longbow in the hands of the English archers was a most formidable weapon. But that was not so much because of the weapon itself as the way it was used. First, let's examine the bow itself and the physics of archery.

The longbow was not invented in the Middle Ages. It dates from the Stone Age. Examples exactly like the medieval long-bow have been dug out of bogs in northern Europe, where the tannic acid has preserved wood that would otherwise have rotted away centuries earlier. No short bows from that era have been found, because they never existed.

Of course, this depends on how short "short" is. Tarassuk and Blair in their *Encyclopedia of Arms and Weapons* say of the Norman bows, "Theirs was a simple weapon, quite small, be-ing only about 1 1/2 meters (5 feet) in length...."[1] It should be noted that none of those Norman bows has ever been found.

In the 1920s, a California physician who was also an ar-chery enthusiast, Dr. Saxton T. Pope, made a replica of a long-bow found on a 16th-century English warship, the *Mary Rose*, which sank in 1545 and was raised in 1841. The bow stave was 6 feet, 4 3/4 inches long. Because it had spent three centuries underwater, no one had ever tried to shoot it. That bow and another from the *Mary Rose* were the only surviving longbows from the period of the longbow's glory. Dr. Pope, an accom-plished bowyer as well as an archer, selected a prime piece of yew, the choice material for longbows, and made a perfect replica of the shipwrecked bow. When he shot it, he found that the draw weight was only 52 pounds and it could shoot a flight arrow only 185 yards.

"To test whether or not this bow might not improve in cast [effective range]," Dr. Pope wrote, "it was cut down to a length of 6 feet. It now weighed 62 pounds and shot the Ishi flight arrow 227 yards. We know, of course, from Toxophilus that the standard English bow was cut down from these stock lengths to suit the size and strength of the archer who shot them. The average bow was the height of a man and his arrow was three quarters of the standard yard, or about 28 inches.'[2] Pope then trimmed the bow to his own height. Its weight rose to 70 pounds and it shot the flight arrow 245 yards.

The reason for this increase in performance was that the shorter the bow, the sharper the curve it was bent into during a full draw. That increased both the weight of the draw and the lightness of the limbs.

Unfortunately, few of the historians who wrote about the longbow have ever shot an arrow with *any* kind of bow. Even fewer understand the physics of archery, which is not complicated, but sometimes seems contradictory. For example, length does not, of itself, give a bow power. If you have two bows of equal "weight" (a measure of the strength it takes to draw the bowstring), equal elasticity, and equal length of draw, the shorter bow will give the arrow more velocity. That's because the limbs of the longer bow are heavier and therefore slower to return to their normal position after having been bent. The catch here is that the bows must have equal weight, elasticity, and length of draw. A short all-wood bow (what archers call a "self bow") could not efficiently shoot an arrow as long as one from a long bow. It would break first. Wood is a relatively brittle material. That's why there never have been short wooden self bows in Europe. Scholars who cite the Bayeux Tapestry as evidence of the mythical short should take another look at that famous cloth: The Norman archers are using bows as long as those their descendants bent two or three centuries later.

Even the most primitive Stone Age archer probably knew instinctively that the farther you pulled the bowstring (assuming the bow didn't break) the farther the arrow would go. That's because, given bows of equal elasticity or resilience, the heavier the draw weight of the bow and the longer distance the bowstring pushes the arrow, the faster the arrow will travel. The English archers typically held the bow in one hand, usually the left, and with the other hand drew the string to the corner of the jaw (or the ear, as some put it). For most men, that was a distance of about 28 inches (a "cloth yard") or 30 inches. An arrow could be longer than that, of course, but any length that extended beyond the front of the bow was dead weight and detracted from the speed and range of the arrow.

Some Native American tribes, who hunted buffalo from horseback, used shorter bows because they couldn't use as long a draw as the English infantrymen. But most of them also backed their shorter bows (between 5 and 5 1/2 inches long) with sinew to keep them from breaking.[3] The Japanese samurai, at the other extreme, used bows between 7 and 8 feet long, but they held the bowstring with the thumb, which allowed them to draw it to a point well behind the head. And the samurai shot these enormous bows from horseback. They were able to do so because the grip on the bow, instead of being in the middle, as it is on most bows, was a third of the length from the bottom.[4]

The weight of the arrow was another factor to be considered. Archers interested in setting records, whether modern sportsmen or medieval Turks, have used especially light missiles called flight arrows. The light arrow achieves much higher velocity and therefore greater range. Arrows for business—hunting or war—were heavier. They had less velocity but more momentum, giving them greater penetration.

Historians have frequently been influenced by the East Roman historian Procopius, who said the Roman archers were superior to their enemies, such as the Goths, because the Romans drew their bowstrings to the ear, whereas their enemies drew them only to the chest. Statements such as that demonstrate nothing more than ignorance of practical archery. The difference in length of draw to the ear or the chest would amount to, at most, about two inches, and if the archer is shooting at a very high angle, as the Norman archers at Hastings did, drawing to the chest is more convenient.

There weren't many other archers in medieval Europe. Most European warriors depended on shock weapons, such as lances, spears, swords, and axes. The North Welsh, who lived in a mountainous country mostly unsuitable for cavalry, had never stopped using long wooden bows. Neither had the Vikings; bows had always been prime weapons for seafarers. And the Normans, of course, had once been called Northmen. Fortunately for Duke William, his people had not entirely forgotten the ways of their ancestors.

What the English *did* do was exploit the bow as a weapon to a far greater extent than any other western Europeans. First, they ensured that there would always be enough highly trained archers. The law required "every Englishman and every Irishman living among Englishmen and speaking English" to own a bow and practice with it every Sunday after church services. For people to practice shooting every week from the time they were growing boys guaranteed a large number of excellent marksmen. It also guaranteed many archers capable of handling a powerful bow. The longbows of that period averaged 75 to 100 pounds draw weight and could shoot a flight arrow a maximum of 290 yards.[5]

The law requiring archery practice continued into the reign of Henry VIII, but Henry inadvertently initiated the decline of English archery. He required that every man older than 25 must shoot at targets 200 or more yards away. He did this because the English military had long specialized in long-range archery. The trouble was that it's hard to see what your arrow has done from 200 yards. Archery stopped being as much fun, and Englishmen began skipping archery practice. That didn't matter much, though; guns had started replacing bows and crossbows in a big way.

To practice long-range archery, the English invented clout (cloth) shooting, in which the target was a large piece of cloth laid flat on the ground. Some sort of marker, like a post, showed the archer where the cloth was. The archer then shot at a high angle to drop his arrow into the cloth. Standing near the cloth was another man, a human target marker. If the arrow hit the cloth, the target marker fell down.

Clout shooting and Henry VIII's statute show that the English were convinced of the value of long-range, high-angle shooting—"plunging fire" in modern terminology. It worked for William the Conqueror, and it worked again at Crecy. No Norman archer at Hastings aimed an arrow at King Harold's eye, but if a shower of arrows fall on thickly massed soldiers, some of those soldiers are bound to be hit. The mercenary

Genoese crossbowmen at Crecy had never faced massed archery before. They took up a position at what was a comfortable range for them—not extreme long range. The largest part of the English army were archers. The Genoese were a small part of the French army. In other words, the archers greatly outnumbered the crossbowmen. The English not only had far more missile troops, but they also had a weapon with a higher rate of fire: The archers could shoot about six shots a minute, the crossbowmen about four shots.[6] Before the Genoese could fire many bolts, they were caught in a storm of arrows—more arrows than they could imagine. They fled. This shooting at Crecy was not, as it is frequently said to be, a test of the effectiveness of the longbow versus the crossbow. It simply showed that in an exchange of missiles, the side with the most missiles wins.

The French knights who followed the Genoese had no missiles at all. They charged, and the storm of arrows swept over them, striking down knights and especially their horses. The charge turned into pandemonium. The archers were shooting from behind a hedge of sharpened stakes designed to break up a cavalry charge, but the French knights were not interested in them. The archers weren't gentlemen. The French knights concentrated on the dismounted English knights in the center of the line.

English archers inflicted another defeat on the French at Agincourt. The English were now convinced that they had the ultimate weapon and ignored developments in weaponry on the continent. But in fact, they didn't even have the best bow. The best bow was the Turkish composite bow, the ultimate development of the Eurasian nomads' basic weapon. The Turkish bow was short and light, making it a good weapon for horsemen.

It consisted of a thin wood core with a belly (the part facing the archer) of horn and a back (the part facing the target) of sinew. Horn has great elasticity when compressed, and sinew does when stretched. Some Turkish bows were copied in Italy, but not many; Europeans were turning to gunpowder weapons.

In 1797, long after the bow's day as a military weapon, English sportsmen got a good look at the Turkish bow. The secretary of the Turkish ambassador gave an exhibition of archery, and he shot a flight arrow 482 yards. "The Toxophilites were astonished, I can tell you," a witness wrote. He said that the longest English shot he had ever heard of was 335 yards, and the most accomplished archer among the witnesses said he had never been able to send a flight arrow beyond 283 yards. The Turk, however, was disappointed. He said both he and his bow were stiff from lack of practice, and that he had seen the Sultan shoot an arrow 800 yards.[7]

The English longbow was seldom if ever pitted against the Turkish composite bow. The English archers, however, frequently fought enemies using the crossbow. King Richard the Lionhearted, in fact, was killed by a shot from a crossbow. Originally, the crossbow had a short wooden bow with a pull weight so heavy the archer had to stand on the bow or a stirrup on the front of the stock and pull the string with both hands. Its missile, called a "bolt," was a short, heavy arrow. The strength of the bow was much greater than that of the longbow, but the draw was much shorter and the bolt much heavier than the longbow's arrow. The short draw detracted from the crossbow's velocity, as did the bolt's weight, but the weight of the missile also improved its penetration. It's hard at this time to estimate the effectiveness of these primitive crossbows, but a Church council decreed that the crossbow was unfit for use against Christians, though not against Muslims. The decree

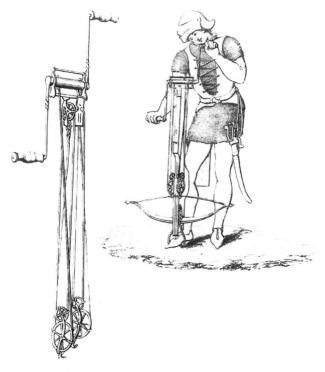

Medieval crossbowman and his weapon. The
crossbow, which was so strong it had to be drawn
with a windlass, greatly outranged the longbow.

was widely ignored. Many thought that Richard's death was
fitting because he was a great advocate of the crossbow.

Later crossbows used steel bows with enormous draw
weights—usually more than a thousand pounds. The bows
were drawn by mechanical devices, such as a windlass or a lever-
and-gear device called a cranequin. Sir Ralph Payne-Gallwey,
a wealthy Englishman with an interest in obsolete weapons,

tested a number of these steel-bowed crossbows and found that their range was far superior to that of the longbow. With one of these crossbows, he shot a bolt 440 to 450 yards, or a bit more than a quarter of a mile.[8]

The French had once said that archery was a gift from God to the English, and so there was no use trying to turn their own peasants into rivals of the English. But the real reason, of course, was that French aristocrats didn't want to be living with peasants who could knock them out of their saddles with a cheap weapon. So they developed their own revolutionary weapon—field artillery. Mobile artillery could appear before castle walls without any preparation. More important, it could demolish the archers and their hedges of stakes from distances far beyond the range of any bow. And so, in the end, the French won the Hundred Years' War.

Against the French and the Scots, the longbow gave the English a great advantage, because their enemies had no comparable missile weapon—or, in the case of the Genoese crossbowmen, no comparable number of missile weapons. But compared with other military bows of the Middle Ages—the Central Asian composite bow, the crossbow, and the Japanese bow—the English longbow was hardly sensational.

MYTH #6

The World's Biggest Guns Reduced Constantinople

The capture of Constantinople by the Turks is considered, along with the discovery of America by Columbus, to signal the end of the Middle Ages and the beginning of the modern world. In 1492, Columbus discovered a new world—a world only a few Europeans, such as the Scandinavians of Iceland, knew existed. But the fall of Constantinople in 1453 renewed Europe's acquaintance with a very old world, one that many of them had forgotten. Scholars from the Greek city flooded into Italy, refueling the renaissance that had already begun there. Greek was again taught in schools, and students learned about times, arts, and sciences that flourished long before classical Rome. Knowledge of that ancient world then spread throughout Europe.

The fall of Constantine's city also showed the world that a new age of warfare had begun in Europe. For more than a thousand years, Constantinople had resisted besiegers—Goths, Huns, Avars, Bulgars, Vikings, Russians, Persians, Magyars, and Arabs. It had been taken only once, by warriors of the misdirected Fourth Crusade, led by the devious, brilliant, blind, 80-year-old Doge of Venice, Enrico Dandolo. The city that had been a dam holding back Muslim hordes had fallen to the Turks.

In so doing, it announced the Gunpowder Revolution with a very loud bang. Mehmet (Mohammad) the Conqueror, formally Mehmedt II, had pounded down Constantinople's hitherto impregnable walls with the largest cannons on earth. Historian Dudley Pope calls Mehmet the First Great Gunner in his book, *Guns.*[1] William H. McNeill in his history of military technology, *The Pursuit of Power*, mentions the Turkish artillery knocking down the walls several times.[2] Many books assert that Mehmet's huge guns made possible the conquest of Constantinople. Pope says that as the guns were about to fire, "It was one of the great historic moments of history because, apart from the fact that Mohammad the Turk was standing at the gateway of Europe with thirteen great guns and fifty-six smaller cannon beside him, artillery was about to win its first decisive victory."[3]

But that isn't true.

The true story is more interesting.

Constantinople, the dam holding back the Muslims, was something like the Hoover Dam in the United States, which holds back the water forming Lake Meade, but releases some of it to generate power. In spite of the Christian roadblock at Constantinople, the Ottoman Empire managed to wage war on the Christian nations of eastern and central Europe. That's because there were Christians, and then there were Christians: The religion of the Eastern Roman Empire was

**The city of Constantinople. The Turks pounded its
walls with the world's largest guns, but took it by
sneaking through an unguarded postern gate.**

Greek Orthodox. The religion of Hungary, for example, was
Roman Catholic. Constantinople allowed Turks fighting one
of the Catholic powers to ferry its troops into Europe for a
fee—a ducat a soldier.

That cost annoyed Mehmet when he became sultan.
Mehmet was no ignorant barbarian. He spoke Turkish, Greek,
Latin, Arabic, Chaldean, and Slavonic. He was a keen student of history, but he was no ivory-tower scholar either. His
Janissaries (household troops and bodyguards) called him "the
drinker of blood." His first act on becoming sultan was to have
an assassin kill his baby brother and thus eliminate a possible
rival. He then killed the assassin. The only Christian he admired was the Count of Transylvania, known to his contemporaries as Vlad the Impaler and to us as Dracula.

Mehmet's first move against Constantinople was to land troops on the European shore of the Bosphorus north of the city and build a fort. The guns of the fort commanded the narrow waterway and cut off the city from the fertile north shore of the Black Sea, where Constantinople, like ancient Athens, got much of its food.

Mehmet had studied developments in artillery and had great faith in guns. Mehmet's chief of ordnance was a renegade Christian named Urban or Orban, variously identified as a Hungarian, a Greek, or a Dane. Knowing the strength of Constantinople, Urban designed cannons that were larger than anything seen before. They were made of bronze and weighed 37 tons. The difficulty of moving such monsters in the 15th century was such that Urban recommended that they be cast on the spot—in front of Constantinople while the siege was under way. Mehmet had many of his smaller bronze cannons melted down to make the big ones.

The cannons were in two pieces with a breech section that screwed to the barrel. The breech section, which held the powder (several hundred pounds of it), and where the charge would explode, had extremely thick walls. The projectile was a stone ball weighting more than 14,000 pounds. The difficulty of loading these enormous cannons was such that one could fire only seven times a day.

Constantinople, as Urban and Mehmet knew, would be a tough nut to crack. The city was on a peninsula, and a wall came right up to the edge of the sea. On the land side, there were three walls: The outermost was a high embankment behind a moat 60 feet wide and 15 feet deep. In 1204, the whole crusading army failed to get by the land walls.

Dandolo's Venetian navy attacked the sea wall but was driven back until its octogenarian doge wrapped himself in the Venetian flag and yelled, "Put me ashore, you craven dogs." But Venice had an enormous navy. Mehmet did not. The Turks would attack the land walls.

Mehmet did have an enormous army, though—much bigger than Constantinople's. Mehmet's 200,000 men included 12,000 Janissaries, the best infantry in that part of the world, if not the planet. The East Roman emperor, Constantine XI, tried to get help from the West. He even agreed to accept the leadership of the Pope. That outraged his own people. With 25,000 men of military age in Constantinople, only 5,000 were willing to fight the Turks. The Pope sent 200 men and another two or three thousand volunteers joined them. The most valuable of them were Giovanni Giustiani of Genoa, a famous commander, and Johann Grant, a German (sometimes identified as Scottish) engineer. All together, Constantine had only one man for each 18-foot section of wall, if he spread them all evenly and nobody slept.

The Turkish troops attacked Constantine's outposts, in one case driving out the garrison with burning sulfur (a primitive gas attack). Mehmet had all his captives impaled. There were continuous attacks on the wall, and Giustiani met them with small cannons, matchlock arquebuses, crossbows, catapults, and "wall guns" (small, portable cannons that pivoted on the wall). The wall guns fired five lead balls with each shot. Turkish bodies covered the fields outside the walls, but Mehmet continued the attack.

The Turks dug tunnels to undermine the walls, but Grant had half buried some drums with dried peas on top in the dirt along the sides of the walls. The vibration of digging made the peas dance on the drumheads and showed the defenders where the Turkish miners were so they could dig countermines. Mehmet's men built siege towers higher than the walls, but as they tried to cross a dry ditch, Giustiani's men rolled barrels of gunpowder under them and blew them all up.

Meanwhile, Mehmet was positioning his massive guns, which needed 140 oxen and 200 men to drag them a few feet to firing positions. On April 1, 1453, the bombardment began.

The defenders waited in vain for the Venetian fleet to appear—a Genoese was commanding the defense, and Genoa was a mortal enemy of Venice, so the Venetian Senate debated sending aid until the sailing season had ended.

The Turkish guns fired night and day. Eventually a section of the wall collapsed, but by that time, Grant and his engineers had built a new wall behind it. At that rate it might take the Turks a century to conquer the city.

On May 29, the frustrated sultan ordered an all-out attack by all his troops. Again, the bodies piled up, but this time, one of the bodies was that of Giovanni Giustiani. That caused some confusion among the defending forces, during which some Janissaries found a small, hidden postern gate (designed to allow the defenders to launch sallies against besiegers) that had been left unlocked and unguarded. The Janissaries entered and attacked the defenders from the rear.

The Turks got into the city.

Constantine XI led the defenders in a counter-charge and was killed. There was a massacre of the inhabitants, but Mehmet stopped it and proclaimed that all inhabitants would have all the liberties and privileges they had enjoyed under the East Roman Empire.

Historians, especially those concerned with artillery, concentrated on the size of the Turkish guns. They *were* huge—probably the largest in the world at that time. And they did knock down walls. But they didn't cause the fall of Constantinople. The great city fell because the Turks got in through an unguarded postern gate.

Myth #7

Guns Made Armor Obsolete

This myth has been repeated innumerable times, although it is obviously untrue. Sometimes the speaker or writer of this myth does concede that the steel helmets used in World War I are armor, but "armor" in this context does not include the fancy helmets and breastplates worn by some elite European regiments. That sort of armor is as utilitarian as a plume of feathers.

The plain fact is that real, utilitarian armor was still worn long after guns had come to rule the battlefield. In fact, armor was issued to troops as late as the Revolutionary War, and in the American Civil War some soldiers purchased their own armor, usually consisting of a steel vest worn under the coat. Some of that armor even protected them.

The earliest picture of a cannon, on the Milemete Manuscript of 1326, shows a man in a complete suit of mail igniting the charge in a vase-shaped cannon. The picture was made when mail was still the fashionable attire for a warrior, long before it had been replaced by plate armor. Dudley Pope's book *Guns* is filled with pictures of armored men using artillery and various types of handguns from the Hundred Years' War to the Thirty Years' War and the British Civil War. Use of armor began to die out during the latter two wars. Cavalry retained it longer than infantry—the saber-bearing horsemen got into more hand-to-hand melees with cutting weapons than did the infantry, and they also had horses to bear the weight of the armor. Engineers wore armor longer than any other branch—they often did their work in fixed positions and were too busy digging or chopping to take defensive measures.

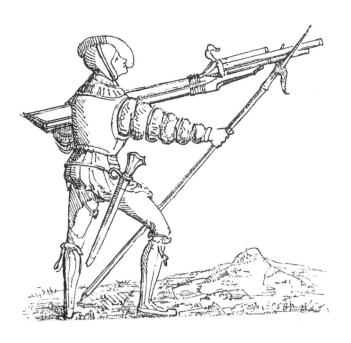

Armored soldier with primitive musket.

Gun fanciers know that guns often bear "proof marks" showing that the weapon was "proofed" by firing it with a charge far heavier than normal. If it did not blow up, that proved that it was safe for normal loads. This practice of proofing was first done with armor, back before there were any guns: The armorer would shoot at his handiwork with a powerful crossbow, and if the crossbow bolt didn't penetrate the plate armor, the

Armored soldier with a later-model musket. Armor was worn by some soldiers into the 20th century and was revived during World War I.

armorer left the dent in place to show that it would resist cross-bow shots. Several years ago, the National Rifle Association conducted a test using antique armor and modern pistols, in which the armor proved to be surprisingly protective.

During the Wars of Religion in the 16th and 17th centuries, German mercenary cavalrymen called Reiters wore full suits of plate armor and were armed almost entirely with wheel-lock pistols—two to six pistols per man. They were organized to fight what had almost become the ultimate weapon of those days, the phalanx of pikemen. The pike phalanx changed the armored cavalryman, such as the knight, from any army's main striking force to an auxiliary. The infantry pike was longer than any lance a horseman could manage, so the old-fashioned cavalry charge would result in the charger, or even the rider being impaled on a pike before his lance could touch the infantry-man. The Reiters responded to the phalanx by abandoning their lances and replacing them with pistols. They used them in an attack called a caracole, in which the horsemen formed a long column and trotted up to the phalanx. Just out of pike range, they fired their pistols and trotted to the rear, reloading as they rode.

The answer to the Reiters' pistols was the musket, a large, heavy hand weapon that had to be fired from a forked stick called a musket rest. Its range was much greater than a pistol and it was powerful enough to penetrate most armor. Of course, armor could be made heavier, but the weight of the latest armor was a serious handicap now that campaigns had become longer and covered much more territory. Soldiers became content with a helmet, a corselet, and a "buff coat" (a coat of thick buffalo leather). Many of them even did without the metal corselet. Civilian hats came to replace helmets, although many of these hats were reinforced with steel bands in the lining. As armor disappeared, the huge musket shrank to the size of the "Brown Bess" carried by both sides in the American Revolution.

British heavy cavalry wore steel cuirasses in Queen Anne's War (1702–14). It was revived for a short period in 1758, then disappeared entirely. Engineers in both the British and French armies continued to wear armor, however. In 1776, a French officer, the Chevalier de Valliere, recommended armor for any troops attacking a fortified place.[1]

A few years ago, workmen repairing historic Fort Ticonderoga on the Hudson found a steel backplate embedded in the walls. It was apparently placed there as a bit of "sympathetic magic," in the belief that a protective spirit in the armor would defend the walls.[2] Another group who wore armor in the Revolution was ship captains. John Paul Jones' armor is preserved at the U.S. Naval Academy.

Privately purchased armor was available long after governments stopped issuing it, but it wasn't popular. It could be extremely uncomfortable during long marches, which were common during the American Civil War. Individual gunmen sometimes sported steel vests long after the Civil War. Wyatt Earp was said to have had one.[3] During the 1920s and 1930s—the age of big gang wars and motorized bank robbers—"bullet proof" vests became rather popular in some circles. By that time, though, military armor had started to make a comeback. In World War I, the heavy use of plunging fire with shrapnel shells—the best way to attack an entrenched enemy—made all belligerents adopt the steel helmet. There was little movement on the Western Front, and the operators of heavy machine guns moved less than other troops, which led the Germans to adopt, on a limited scale, body armor for machine gunners.

There was much more movement in World War II, and armor appeared for the most mobile of warriors—aircraft crews. They wore flak jackets (FLAK is an acronym for *flieger abwehr kanone*, German for "antiaircraft gun). The primary purpose of the jacket was to protect the wearer from fragments of exploding antiaircraft shells. Infantrymen had holes to hide in, but the air crews were totally exposed up in the sky.

In the latter part of the Korean War, a trench war like World War I, the ground pounders got the equivalent of flak jackets. Similar to the aircraft garment, these were worn to protect soldiers from shell fragments. The author remembers one incident when the jackets were distributed: A soldier put on the sleeveless jacket and handed his carbine to another man.

"Shoot me," he said. "I'm bulletproof!"

His comrades persuaded him to test the armor first. They hung it on the remains of a blasted sapling and fired at it. The carbine bullet went through the front of the jacket, the blasted tree, and the back of the jacket, and continued on to parts unknown.

Today, soldiers in Iraq and Afghanistan wear much better armor. These jackets will stop bullets from an ordinary rifle, although probably not from one of the .50-caliber sniper rifles now in use.

Far from becoming obsolete, since the time of the Greek hoplites, armor has never totally disappeared (though it has never provided total protection either). Armored warriors have been dying in battle for thousands of years.

MYTH #8

The *Monitor* and the *Merrimack* Staged the First Ironclad Duel

The CSS *Virginia*, reconstructed from the USS *Merrimack,* steamed into Hampton Roads March 9, 1862, to complete the destruction of blockading Union warships. The *Virginia* was an odd-looking craft. Her hull had been cut down to a short distance above the waterline, and where the rest of the hull had been were sloping sides covered with iron plates and pierced with ports for cannons. When she first appeared, the *Virginia* had an iron beak fixed to her bow, like the ram of an ancient galley. She was the first of a new class of warships called "rams" that were used, it turned out, exclusively by the Confederacy. The *Virginia* lost her ram when she hit the USS *Cumberland*, but the *Cumberland* sank in minutes with a hole in her hull "big enough to drive a horse and cart through," according to a witness.[1] Undeterred by the loss of her ram, the *Virginia* went after the USS *Congress* and drove her onto the shore in a hail of gunfire. Another

Union ship, the USS *Minnesota*, hastening to aid the *Congress*, ran ashore. Darkness saved her, but the Confederate ironclad came out the next day to finish the job.

The *Monitor* and the *Virginia* (nee *Merrimack*) slug it out centuries after the first fight between ironclads.

There she met an even stranger-looking ship. The newcomer's deck was almost at the waterline and she had no superstructure but a round turret mounting two large Dahlgren guns and a pilot post near the bow, a tiny box about big enough for a human head. Like the *Virginia*, the new craft, the USS *Monitor*, was armored with iron plates.

The epic slugging match of the two ships ended in a draw, but it has always been remembered as the first battle of naval ironclads in history.

It's remembered that way in the United States, that is, but that's because of the way "world history" is taught in secondary schools. The average high school student learns about the

Stone Age, when people lived crudely but invented fire; about the ancient world, when people crawled out of their caves and began building pyramids; and about the classical age, when the Greeks invented philosophy and carved statues of naked people while the Romans fed other people to the lions. Then the student gets to the history of European nations—western European nations, that is—and learns about Columbus and the history of North America, barely noting the existence of any nation south of the Rio Grande, and precious little about Canada. The student learns nothing about the Far East between Peking Man and the 15th century, until being taught that the Portuguese, Dutch, English, and French were trying to corner trade with the East Asian countries.

Some kids learned that gunpowder was probably invented in China and that China and Japan also learned a bit about Western technology. Very few learned that after generations of internal strife, a certain Toyotomi Hideyoshi became the de facto ruler of Japan. The theoretical ruler of Japan was the emperor, but the *actual* ruler was a military commander called a shogun. Hideyoshi could not be a shogun, because he was a commoner—the first and only commoner in the history of Japan to reach the top of the social order. But Hideyoshi did bring peace.

For him, peace grew out of the barrel of a gun—in this case the matchlock harquebus introduced to Japan by some Portuguese sailors. The great noble whom Hideyoshi had served, Oda Nobunaga, saw the value of matchlocks and used them widely in wars with other nobles. According to Noel Perrin, "At least in Japan in absolute numbers, guns were almost certainly more common in Japan in the late sixteenth century than in any other country in the world."[2] Oda almost succeeded in unifying Japan, but he died in the wars. Hideyoshi took his place and finished the job.

Hideyoshi was not an imposing figure. Behind his back, people called him "Old Monkey Face," but he had unlimited ambition. Having ended Japan's seemingly endless civil war, he decided to conquer China. The best way to get to China was through Korea, so Hideyoshi sent envoys to the King of Korea to ask for free passage of his army to China. King Son Jo and his court laughed at the Japanese, but it was not wise to laugh at Toyotomi Hideyoshi.

The Korean armed forces (in Korea at the time, the army and navy were the same service) had not been at war for many years. The Korean fighters were much less numerous than the Japanese and their handguns were far inferior in both numbers and quality to the Japanese harquebuses. They did have something new, though: vessels called "turtle ships," or kobukson. They were similar to the panokson, the standard Korean warship, except that the sides of the hull were protected with iron plates.

The turtle ship was 34.2 meters long and 10.3 meters wide. On its bow was a dragon's head, and firing through the dragon's mouth was a cannon. The stern of the ship was shaped like a turtle's tail, and beneath the tail was another cannon. The ship had two decks. On the lower deck were oarsmen. There were eight oars on each side. In combat, five oarsmen would pull each oar, but other times pairs of oarsmen would take turns. Above the oar deck was the gun deck, with six cannons on each side. Below the dragon's head on the bow was a metal gargoyle head right at the waterline that served as a ram. A favorite Korean tactic was to ram an enemy ship, and then, as the rowers backed water, fire the dragon's head cannon into the breach. Flaming arrows could also be shot through the dragon's head, and smoke could be projected through the dragon's mouth to lay down a smoke screen.[3]

Japanese naval tactics, on the other hand, were primarily based on boarding. Japanese ships had few cannons (although the Japanese had far more handguns than the Koreans). To counter boarders, the Korean ships had roofs over the upper deck that were studded with sharp iron spikes, sometimes concealed by straw mats. Both the armored kobukson and the unarmored panukson had flat bottoms so they could be driven right up to the beaches lining Korea's extensive tidelands.[4] The flat bottom also allowed the Korean ships to change direction by swiveling in place. The Japanese ships with round bottoms and keels were faster but had a much wider turning circle.

The Korean turtle ships' armor was not unique either. In 1578, the Japanese had several ships commissioned by Oda Nobunaga that were 36 meters long, 21 meters wide, and covered with iron plates.[5] It is not known whether these ships were used in the invasion of Korea, but it seems unlikely that such formidable craft would be left behind, especially considering the disasters that befell the Japanese navy during that operation. It seems virtually certain that the first clash of ironclads happened almost 300 years before the *Virginia* and the *Monitor* traded shots.

Iron armor was not, then, the major Korean advantage. Korea's ace in the hole was a human being, Yi Sun-sin. Admiral Yi had helped design the turtle ships, and when the war broke out, he was commander of a large portion of the Korean fleet.

On April 14, 1592, Hideyoshi landed 160,000 troops at Pusan, the southern port well remembered by all American veterans of the 1950–53 Korean War. The Japanese routed the poorly equipped Korean soldiers, and 18 days after landing in Korea, the Japanese reached Seoul. Son Jo fled.

Admiral Yi had been busy, though. He got his fleet together—only 27 ships at first—and began attacking Japanese convoys. On May 7, he attacked 26 Japanese ships and sank all of them. The same day he fell on five other Japanese ships and sank all of them as well. The next day, he found 13 enemy ships and sank 11 of them. By June 7, he had increased his fleet to 51 ships and fought seven battles, winning all of them. In each battle, he had outnumbered the enemy, but in July, he planned to take on a much larger fleet.

To destroy the bothersome Korean navy, Hideyoshi sent 73 ships to Korea. Yi learned that the Japanese were anchored in the Kyonnaeryang Channel, a narrow waterway filled with sunken rocks. Yi decided there wasn't enough room to maneuver, and the sunken rocks made any maneuvering dangerous. He combined his fleet with another admirals and stationed 56 warships near Hansan-do, an island near Koje-do, site of a huge POW camp in the 1950–53 war. The Korean warships were in a formation called the Crane Wing, a semicircle facing the mouth of the channel. Yi sent five of his wooden ships up the channel. When the Japanese saw the five Korean ships, they hauled up their anchors and dashed at them. The Korean ships swiveled and headed down the channel at full speed.

When the Japanese got within sight of Hansan-do, they found themselves surrounded on three sides by Yi's Crane Wing. Of the 73 Japanese warships, 47 were sunk and 12 were captured. Only 14 got away.

Hideyoshi then forbade his forces to engage in naval battles with the Koreans. A British naval historian, Vice Admiral George A. Ballard, in his *The Influence of the Sea on the Political History of Japan,* writes of the battle of Hansan-do: "This was the great Korean admiral's crowning exploit. In the short space of six weeks he had achieved a series of successes unsurpassed in the whole annals of maritime war, destroying the enemy's battle fleets, cutting his lines of communications, sweeping up his convoys...and bringing his ambitious schemes to utter ruin. Not even Neson, Blake or Jean Bart could have done more than this scarcely known representative of a small and cruelly oppressed nation."[6]

The victory encouraged China to enter the war. The Japanese retreated from the Yalu. Two months after the Battle of Hansan-do they abandoned Seoul. Yi was promoted to commander of all Korean naval forces. Hideyoshi began negotiations to end the war. In 1596, however, the negotiations broke down and Hideyoshi came up with a new plan to get rid of Yi Sun-sin. A Japanese named Yoshira came to a Korean general and offered him valuable information about the Japanese forces. A little later, he said the Japanese would again invade Korea and told the Korean, General Kim Eung-su, where the landing would take place. Kim passed the information to King Son Jo, who ordered Yi to attack the Japanese. Yi knew the water around the landing spot was filled with submerged rocks. Any naval maneuvers there would be suicidal, he said. He refused to move.

Hideyoshi probably knew of Yi's fear of submerged rocks and thought this would be a painless way to get rid of him. He almost did.

The king thought Yi's refusal was pure arrogance. He had the admiral arrested and tortured. Only the pleas of court officials, who remembered Yi's victories, saved him from death. The admiral was reduced in rank from commander of all naval forces to the lowest private in the army. His place was taken by a longtime rival, Won Kyun. Won took Korea's 168 ships to fight Japan's 500, later 1,000, warships. The fighting lasted three days. On the first, Won lost seven ships, on the second, 27 ships, and on the third, 134 ships. His fleet was annihilated. He swam ashore and was killed by a Japanese soldier.

The king reinstated Yi Sun-sin.

On September 16, 1597, Yi took Korea's remaining warships—all 13 of them—against a Japanese fleet of 330. They met in a channel too narrow for all of the Japanese ships to deploy, but 130 managed to surround Yi's 13. Japan's boarding tactics were stymied by the Korean artillery and fire arrows; their ships couldn't get close enough to board. Then a Japanese defector who was one of Yi's interpreters recognized the body of the Japanese admiral floating on the blood-stained sea. Yi had the body fished up and hung on a mast so all of the Japanese sailors could see that their leader was dead. Then the current of the channel changed and disrupted the formations of both fleets. The Japanese lost heart and fled up the channel, but Yi had placed iron chains attached to capstans across the channel below the surface. As the Japanese ships passed, Korean troops hauled up the chains and capsized them. All told, 31 Japanese ships were sunk and 90 severely damaged. The ailing Toyotomi Hideyoshi got the news in Osaka Castle. Less than a year later, he was dead. What the Koreans call the Seven Years War was over.

There was one last act, though. Yi and a Chinese admiral, Chien Lien, teamed up to give the departing Japanese ships a sendoff. Korea had 83 ships and China 63. They attacked 500 Japanese ships and sank 450 of them. But Korea paid a heavy price: A bullet from a Japanese matchlock took the life of Yi Sun-sin. The Korean admiral had fought 23 battles and never lost one. In fact, he never lost one ship. No other admiral has such a record.

The history of the Far East at the time of the European Renaissance is little known in the United States, so the operations of these first armored warships and the great Admiral Yi, who commanded then, are almost completely forgotten.

MYTH #9

When the Revolution Began, the American Colonists Split Three Ways

This myth is seen frequently even though there is little foundation for it. It was probably invented by a British historian. The British are a bit hazy on American history. A lot of them think the American Civil War concerned such people as George Washington and Benjamin Franklin.[1] That this myth remains current is largely due to ignorance about a distinctly American colonial institution: the militia.

These days when most people hear "militia" they think of political extremists who carry guns and threaten armed revolt in defense of various alleged "rights." Or else they think of the National Guard, an all-volunteer state military organization. Neither of these is the militia mentioned in the second amendment of the U.S. Constitution.

All of the British colonies in what is now the United States had militia laws that included just about all able-bodied males with few exceptions, such as ministers of religion. A person didn't *join* the militia; he automatically became a member as soon as he reached a certain age, such as 16. The militia was a European institution going back to the Middle Ages, but it had been allowed to disappear as regular armies were developed. In the colonies there was always danger of a sudden attack by hostile Native Americans or soldiers from other European colonial powers, such as France. Therefore all men were required to have a musket or a rifle, a prescribed quantity of bullets, flints, and gunpowder. They also had to have a sword, a hatchet, or a bayonet. (The hatchet was the most popular alternative, as the other two were not much use around the house.)

The militia constituted a colony's military power. Many militia outfits had their own artillery. There was some cavalry, but not much in the mountainous, forested Northeast. Militiamen elected their officers and drilled in the European fashion. When fighting Native Americans, though, they often used Native American tactics, such as taking cover behind trees and rocks and advancing by rushes.

British officers had a tendency to laugh at the militia—"amateur soldiers," they said, although the militia had always been their allies. At Concord they got a chance to see the militia from the other side: While the Redcoats were marching out from Boston, word spread by Paul Revere and others was activating a vast militia organization. Revere, for example, did not ride down the streets screaming "The British are coming!" For one thing, he and everybody else considered themselves British. What he said was, "The regulars are out," and he said it to select people: leaders of the Sons of Liberty, the revolutionary organization; influential ministers; and especially militia officers. These people had various ways of calling up the militia, which the British officers who captured Revere saw in action. They heard shots from signal guns and trumpet calls, and they saw waving lanterns and beacon fires. They heard Revere say that those were signs that the country was rising, and if they continued toward Concord they'd be dead men. They released the revolutionary courier, took his horse, and rode back to join the main body of royal troops.

At Concord, the British saw the results of those signals. There were no men of military age in the town, but two regiments of the Middlesex militia were on the other side of the North Bridge, marching to the music of fifes and drums. The tune was the *White Cockade*, the song of the Jacobite Scottish rebels of 1745.

Three companies of British light infantry fired at the militia. The militia fired back and 12 British went down. All the light infantry ran for their lives; eight of the wounded got up and joined them. They left four dead redcoats. At this point the fight was strictly along European lines, but this changed as the British retreated to Boston. Sometimes militia companies lined up and volleyed at the British, but more often they fired from behind trees and stone walls. Militia General William Heath took command and completely surrounded the British, moving ahead of their vanguard and closely following their rear.

It is important to note again that *every* man in Massachusetts was an armed member of the militia. None made any attempt to aid the royal troops, and not one declared that he was neutral. In fact, if a third of the militia were loyalists and another third were neutral, as has been claimed, colonial America would have been the scene of a terrible civil war. It never happened.

There were Tories, of course (loyalists who sided with Britain); some of the upper classes in New York and Philadelphia favored King George, but they were a small minority and kept quiet until the British occupied those cities. Many of them then joined outfits like Banestre Tarleton's British Legion (which was almost entirely American). The western fur traders in what had been Sir William Johnson's fur empire joined his successors, John and Walter Butler, in their Tory Legion; and Sir John Simcoe, one of the founders of British Canada, gathered some back-country Tories for his Tory Rangers. All of these Tories, however, were very much a minority in the North.

There were more Tories in the South, but they were still a minority, although they did include a few genuine militia units. They did not become Tories because they wanted to remain a British colony, however. When talk of independence began, the planters in the eastern Carolinas jumped on the bandwagon—particularly the millionaire rice planters in South Carolina, who felt that England was restricting their trade with Europe. Without British interference, they would quickly become much richer. The small farmers in the Piedmont area didn't like the eastern planters. They had reasons: The eastern planters ran the Carolinas, they appointed magistrates and sheriffs for the whole state, and practically disenfranchised the farmers in the central part of the states. The result was a civil war called the War of Regulation between the "Regulators," militia from the Piedmont, and state government troops. The government won, and, as the easterners were Whigs (those opposed to the royal government), many of the former Regulators became Tories.

If anyone in the colonies were neutral, it would have to have been the "Over Mountain" people in the Big Smokies. They had little to do with either the Piedmont farmers or the eastern planters. But then the British government got the bright idea of stirring the Cherokees up against them. The Over Mountain people soon became ardent Whigs.

The American Long Rifle Was the Best Rifle in the World

There are almost as many lies about the American (also known as the Pennsylvania or Kentucky) long rifle as there are about the English longbow. We have been told that it was capable of fantastic accuracy—the most accurate weapon in the world! It was this weapon, it has been said, that allowed the poor, thinly populated British colonies to gain their independence from the most powerful nation on the planet.

We have been told that the British were not riflemen. That their military small arms were exclusively smoothbores (in which the inside of the barrel did not have any rifling, or grooves to spin the bullet). That there were rifles in Europe, but they were heavy, clumsy things, not at all like the slim, elegant American long rifle. That European riflemen had to pound their bullets down the bore from the muzzle, using an iron ramrod and a wooden mallet, and the grooves in the rifling could cut into the lead bullet, which slowed their rate of fire tremendously. The ingenious Americans, in contrast, wrapped their slightly undersize bullets in a greased patch of cloth, which took the rifling adequately and let the projectile slide down the bore without pounding. Among the "Hessians" (a term applied to all the German troops rented to the British army by their kings and princes) were jägers (hunters) who carried rifles instead of muskets. But the jägers, with their short, clumsy rifles, were no match for the American riflemen.

Most of the above "information" comes not only from patriotic American writers, but from contemporary British officers. Yet it's mostly garbage.

First of all, few Americans, and even few Britons, had ever seen a European rifle in the mid- to late 18th century. When the Revolution began, they did see the jägers' rifles in action. According to Robert Held, an antiquarian and expert on the American long rifle, the jägers were not hunters at all, but "decrepit conscripts sold like cattle and equipped with decrepit, worn-out wrecks of mostly unserviceable rifles."[1] But some of the jägers and their rifles may not have been so decrepit after all. In fact, jäger snipers were said to be a serious threat to the besiegers of Yorktown. George Tucker, a Continental soldier at that siege, reported on the effectiveness of those jäger rifles: "A few shots were fired...from the Enemy's Redoubts.... The Execution was much more than might have been expected from the Distance, the dispersed situation of our Men, and the few shot fired."[2]

There were not that many sharpshooting jägers, however, and British officers became quite impressed with the marksmanship of the American riflemen. One was Major George Hanger, himself an accomplished rifleman. Hanger was no fan of the regulation British musket:

A soldier's musket, if not exceedingly ill-bored (as many of them are), will strike the figure of a man at 80 yards; it may even at 100; but a soldier must be very unfortunate indeed who shall be wounded by a common musket at 150 yards, provided his antagonist aims at him; and as to firing at a man at 200 yards with a common musket, you may just as well fire at the moon and have the same hope of hitting your object. I do maintain and will prove, whenever called on, that no man was ever killed at 200 yards, by a common soldier's musket, by the person who aimed at him.[3]

Being used to such terrible accuracy, Hanger was greatly impressed by the accuracy of the American riflemen on the other side. He was taken prisoner after the Battle of Saratoga, and before he was exchanged, he was able to talk with American riflemen: "I have many times asked the American backwoodsman what the most their best marksmen could do; they have constantly told me that an expert rifleman, provided he can draw a good and true sight...can hit the head of a man at 200 yards."[4]

Hanger recalled an experience of his own: He and Colonel Banestre Tarleton were discussing plans for an attack. Both were mounted, as was their bugler, who was there to signal their troops. An American rifleman appeared and took a prone position about 400 yards from them. He fired, and the bugler said, "Sir, my horse is shot." The animal staggered a few steps, fell down, and died. The bugler had been a little to the rear of the two officers and between them as seen from the rifleman's position. The colonel and major quickly rode back to rejoin their troops.

The American rifle did give a bullet more velocity than its European counterpart. That was necessary because hunting conditions in the Alps and the Pennsylvania woods were quite different. The foothills of the Alps were inhabited by 400-pound, tusked, bad-tempered wild boars given to unprovoked charges. The hunter needed a heavy bullet to stop those beasts, so the jägers carried rifles of .70 or even .85 caliber. Alpine hunting also required a lot of climbing, which is a lot easier with a short rifle than with a long one, especially if it has a sling.

America had grizzly bears, but not in the eastern half of the country. There were black bears, but a hunter didn't need a cannon like the European rifle to stop one of those. He needed lighter ammunition, because hunting in America often involved long trips, far from any civilized town. For an average European rifle, a pound of lead would cast only 10 or 15 bullets, whereas a pound of lead would make 40 or 50 bullets for a long rifle. Bullets of .45 or .50 caliber could take care of black bears as well as a far more dangerous woods denizen, the hostile Native American. These bullets needed less powder to propel them, but that smaller amount of powder could give them more velocity, and hence a flatter trajectory. A flat trajectory was important if the shooter didn't have time to carefully calculate the range to his target. The Alpine hunter usually had plenty of time to do that, but in Native American fighting, quick shooting was often necessary.

It's commonly believed that the long barrel of the American rifle gave it more accuracy. Not so. A mere few inches of barrel give a bullet its direction. Once it's on its way, it will not change direction unless acted upon by an outside force, such as wind or striking a twig. The long barrel does improve the sight radius, but this has little effect when the barrel is more than about 36 inches long. The long barrel was also believed to let the powder burn more completely, giving the bullet more velocity. But actually, in the long rifle, the powder had burned pretty completely before the bullet ever reached the muzzle. At that point the friction of the long barrel on the bullet actually began to retard the bullet before it left the gun.

Major General Julian S. Hatcher, an internationally recognized expert on ordnance, wrote, "Experiments with .22 caliber arms has shown conclusively that little, if any, accuracy or velocity is to be gained by making the barrel longer than 10 inches."[5] Modern studies have shown that the .22 long rifle cartridge actually loses velocity when barrel length exceeds 16 inches. The American long rifle took a heftier powder charge than a modern .22, but black powder burns faster than modern smokeless powder and it was certainly all burned long before the bullet reached the end of a 40-inch barrel.

Fairly early in the history of the American long rifle, gunmakers learned that those ultra-long barrels contributed nothing to the efficiency of the rifle. But their customers still wanted long barrels, so that's what they made.

It should be noted that American long rifles were not issued by any government. They were strictly private property. They were made to order, and they were basically hunting weapons. They did not take bayonets because the men who ordered them did not want bayonets. For hand-to-hand fighting, they used both long sheath knives and hatchets, which were also useful for many day-to-day tasks, whereas bayonets were not. The frontiersmen had no training in bayonet fighting, but they had become quite expert in fighting with the knife or the hatchet.

Let's not forget that patched ball. European rifles made before 1580 have patch boxes in their stocks that contain grease. In 1644, Diego Espinar wrote a book on hunting with rifle and crossbow, called *Arte de Ballesteria y Monteria*, in which he explained in detail the use of a patched ball. In other words, Europeans were using greased patches in their rifles a century before the American long rifle was born, so it wasn't those that made the American rifle more deadly.

Furthermore, the workmanship on American long rifles could not match the European rifles. According to Robert Held, "the makers of even the best examples [of American long rifles] would not have got [sic] their apprentice papers had they submitted a sample to the Munich, Geneva or Vienna rifle maker's guilds."[6] Held described the locks of American rifles as "rough, crude, ill-fitted,"[7] and cited an article by an avid long rifle shooter who boasted of getting off 16 shots before his rifle missed fire; a top-quality London flintlock, Held wrote, could fire a thousand times or more without missing fire.

Regular officers like Mad Anthony Wayne disparaged the American rifle. Wayne said he never wanted to see another rifle, at least not without a bayonet, and even then, he'd prefer a musket.[8] Wayne preferred the musket because its speed of fire was greater than any rifle, even those using the greased patch. The musketeer used paper cartridges containing both powder and shot—usually one large lead ball and several buckshot. He bit one end of the paper cartridge, poured a little powder into the flash pan of the lock, then poured the bulk of the powder down the muzzle and rammed the paper and bullets down after the powder. The rifleman, by contrast, loaded powder from his powder horn, put a greased patch over the muzzle and a bullet over the patch, and rammed them down on top of the powder. Even with a greased patch, the rifle's rate of fire was about one round a minute. He could then only fire a few shots before cleaning the bore, otherwise the charcoal left by the black powder would clog the rifling, making the gun impossible to load.

A smoothbore didn't have that trouble. An English military treatise of the time says that in training a musketeer, "No recruit is to be dismissed from the drill until he is so expert with his firelock as to load and fire fifteen times in three minutes and three quarters."[9] Old soldiers could fire a lot faster.

Nevertheless, the rifle was an important weapon, especially in the semi-guerrilla war in the South. A huge part of the southern militia were riflemen, and they functioned as mounted infantry. On seeing a British infantry formation, they would tie their horses well out of musket range and fire their rifles. If the infantry tried to charge them, they'd mount up and ride back out of range. Britons subjected to these tactics were greatly impressed with the American long rifle, as Major Hanger certainly was. And as a rifleman himself, he could appreciate the talent of the American backwoodsmen. Hanger wasn't the only rifleman in the British army; Major Patrick Ferguson was an even more accomplished rifleman—he was not only the best shot in the British army, but he also invented a superior sort of rifle. The Ferguson Rifle was actually an improvement on a French weapon. It was a breech loader. The rifle's breech block was a thick screw attached to the trigger guard. One turn of the screw opened the breech. The rifleman then put a bullet and powder into the breech. The Ferguson Rifle's rate of fire was much greater than the long rifle's.

Ferguson led a company of snipers at the Battle of Brandywine. At one point in the battle, he had a high-ranking American officer in his sights, but he couldn't bring himself to shoot such a noble-looking man in the back, so he held his fire. A short time later, an American musket ball hit him in the right arm. He lost the use of that arm and the chance to ever fire a rifle again. Evidence indicates that the officer he didn't shoot was George Washington.

Similar to the longbow, which was not the best in the world, the long rifle was not the best rifle in the world. But as with the English and their bows, the Americans had a lot of rifles, and their enemies did not.

Myth #11

American Revolutionary Troops Seldom Fought From Cover

This myth grew from an attempt to correct another misunderstanding about the Revolutionary war—that the Americans *always* hid behind stone walls and trees while the stupid British lined up in the open and fired volleys on command.

Historians have denounced this idea as a myth for years. "Baron von Steuben didn't teach Indian tactics," is a common comment. Unfortunately, that depends on another myth, namely that the Americans frequently lost during the early part of the war, and after Steuben's training at Valley Forge, the rebel army became a winning team. The truth is that the American rebels won more battles, including the decisive one at Saratoga (which convinced France, Spain, and Holland to enter the war against Britain) *before* Steuben's instructions, not after them. Not that Steuben didn't provide an extremely valuable service. He arranged that all units of the army be of uniform strength, which was an invaluable aid to planning, and provided a single, uniform drill book. It's just that the British and German troops they fought were more expert at linear tactics than the Americans.

Of the idea that Americans did most of their firing from behind trees and stone walls, Harold L. Peterson, chief curator of the National Park Service and all national historic sites, as well as author of 19 books on historic weapons and armor, says, "With the exception of King's Mountain and the retreat from Concord, no major battle followed this pattern."[1]

Of course, much depends on what battles you consider "major." And what you mean by "pattern." In quite a few battles, including the Concord campaign, the Americans used both types of tactics.

AMERICAN MARKSMAN UP A TREE.

An American marksman shooting from a tree.

Concord opened with the British light infantry firing from the "street firing" formation. They formed a long column, four abreast. The first rank volleyed and ran to the rear while the second rank fired. This formation made possible a continuous stream of fire down a narrow, built-up 18th-century European street. The trouble was that Concord didn't have narrow, built-up streets, but scattered houses along the narrow lanes. The Middlesex militia, 500 men in a double column, replied with a long, ripping volley that hit 12 of the Redcoats—four fatally—and terrified the rest. So far, everything was very European. The militia even marched to the music of fifes and drums.

Things began to change when Colonel Francis Smith's men began their retreat to Boston. Some militia units stepped out of the woods and fired volleys at the regulars, and others fired from houses, stone walls, and from behind trees. Hezekiah Wyman at 55 was too old to be a minuteman or even a regular militiaman, but he saddled his white mare and rode toward the sound of firing. When he saw the British, he jumped off his horse, laid his musket across the saddle, and shot one of the Redcoats. Then he got back on the horse and rode ahead. He was seen many times that day—a tall, gaunt man with long gray hair on a white horse. Each time he appeared, he shot a soldier, remounted, and rode ahead.

Wyman was much younger than Samuel Wittemore, a badly crippled 78-year-old. When Wittemore heard that the British were coming, he grabbed his musket, two pistols, and a sword, and got behind a stone wall. When the regulars got within range, Wittemore fired five shots so fast that the British thought several men were behind that wall. A British detachment charged the wall. Wittemore killed one soldier with the musket and shot two more with his pistols. He was reaching for his saber when the British shot him, bayoneted him, and left him for dead. He didn't die, though. He lived to be 96.

The British reacted savagely to this sort of resistance. They killed fighters they had taken prisoner. Later, they broke into houses along the road, looted them, burned them, and killed anyone they found in them.

Militia general William Heath took command of the rebel force and surrounded the British column. Heath, like Henry Knox, was a keen theoretical student of war, although he had no practical experience. He did not consider the type of war being fought "barbaric" or "uncouth." The American militia were using light infantry tactics, which had been part of British Army strategy since the French and Indian War. Surrounding the British column with a moving ring of skirmishers ("dispersed tho' adhering," one participant described it) was a classic light infantry tactic, as well as doctrine of such East European semi-guerrillas as the Cossacks, Pandours, and Hussars. Militia troops in front of the British vanguard kept firing all the way back to Charlestown while other troops blasted the column's rear and flanks. Most of the firing was from cover. This sort of fighting was better adapted to forested, rocky country like most of eastern America, whereas straight lines of soldiers firing rapid volleys were most effective in open spaces, such as the farms and pastures Europeans were used to.

There was little militia cavalry in New England because of the terrain. Some of it got into the Concord fight, but they fought like mounted infantry instead of cavalry, dismounting and firing muskets at the Redcoats, then remounting and taking up positions farther ahead, waiting for the enemy to come within range.

General Gage, learning that things were not going as planned, sent his subordinate, Lord Percy, with reinforcements and two field pieces to rescue Smith's column. His lordship was in such a hurry that he neglected to take along extra ammunition. Gage sent six wagons, driven by grenadiers, to give Percy the ammunition he needed. They were met by members of an "alarm company," militamen too old for first-line duty. The grenadiers laughed at the old geezers who were trying to stop them, especially as they were led by an old black man. The old black man, David Lamson, gave an order and the over-the-hill warriors shot the lieutenant in charge, two sergeants, and one horse in each wagon team. The grenadiers ran for their lives and surrendered to the first person they saw: an old woman working in her garden.

There were three types of revolutionary soldiers: Continentals, who were paid by the Continental Congress; the state line, who were paid by the states; and the militia, who were not paid. But at this stage of the war, there was only the militia. The Continentals were the best trained; the militia the least trained. Most of the training had been in standard European linear tactics, mostly because they were easier to teach. When a fight got hot, the militia tended to forget their training and do what came naturally, which was, after all, the basis of the newly developed light infantry tactics.

The Battle of Bennington, a preliminary to the decisive Battle of Saratoga, was fought entirely by militia on the American side, and by German "Hessians" (actually Brunswickers), some Tories in British service, and some Canadian Native Americans on the other. As it was part of the Saratoga campaign, Peterson may not have considered it a "major" battle, but the Americans fired while moving from tree to tree, while the Germans tried to dress their lines in the woods and fire volleys.

Burgoyne, moving down from Canada, had sent these troops into the woods to gather supplies and, above all, recruit the Tories he believed were thick on the ground. He didn't get any supplies and his men didn't find any Tories. The Native Americans ran at almost the first shots and went back to Canada. The Germans fought bravely but were virtually annihilated. Burgoyne lost 15 percent of his regular soldiers in this "minor" engagement.

George Washington had nothing against his soldiers fighting from cover. He said, "Place them behind a parapet, a breastwork, a stone wall, or any other thing that will afford them shelter, and from their knowledge of a firelock, they will give a good account of their enemy.... But I am as well convinced, as if I had seen it, that they will not march boldly up to a work or stand in a plain." And so, he said, "I have never spared the spade and the pickaxe."[2]

The New England "cavalry" in the Concord campaign, and especially the Southern mounted riflemen mentioned in the last chapter, used distance and mobility to give them protection. The country was more open in much of the South, with large farms and wide pastures. There were forests, mountains, and swamps, though, and guerrilla leaders like Francis "the Swamp Fox" Marion used that terrain as efficiently as their Northern comrades used theirs.

At times, as at Guilford Courthouse, linear tactics were most appropriate. Most of the soldiers at Saratoga—British, Continental, state line, and militia—used linear tactics. Benedict Arnold's men did when he led them in a charge that took the Breymann redoubt. Daniel Morgan's riflemen didn't. They couldn't; their rifles had no bayonets. They filtered through the woods in response to orders Morgan gave them with a turkey call instead of a bugle.

At a crucial point in the battle, Brigadier Simon Fraser appeared to be rallying the fading British. Morgan called his best marksman, Tim Murphy, and pointed to Fraser. "Kill that officer," he said. Murphy climbed a tree (no small trick while holding a 10-pound, 5-foot-long rifle), and fired. The first shot passed through the mane of Fraser's horse. Murphy had a double-barrel rifle. He released a catch and rotated the barrels. His second shot chipped a piece off Fraser's saddle. Fraser's staff officers begged him to make himself less conspicuous. The brigadier said generals were supposed to be conspicuous. Murphy reloaded and fired again. He hit Fraser in the abdomen. His aides took the Scottish officer off the battlefield, and the British line collapsed.

Perhaps the most purely guerrilla-type battle of the war was at King's Mountain, where another Scottish commander was killed by a rifleman. The unfortunate officer was Major Patrick Ferguson, the great rifleman who could no longer use his favorite weapon. Ferguson was one of the few British aristocrats who could charm ordinary people. He was in charge of raising a Tory militia in the Carolinas and had been remarkably successful. The rifleman talked to other riflemen who felt oppressed by the rich planters of the East Coast. Whig leaders thought Ferguson was more dangerous than the ruthless Banestre "Bloody Ban" Tarleton. Ferguson perpetrated no massacres like Tarleton and hanged no civilians like other British leaders, but he tried to intimidate the Whigs (those opposed to the Crown) in the Smoky Mountains by threatening to lay waste to their land.

The "Over Mountain" men decided they had to get rid of Ferguson. They got their rifles and horses and set out. They cornered Ferguson and his American Tories on King's Mountain. Ferguson knew all about using a rifle, but almost nothing about how to use a large group of riflemen. He had his men whittle down the handles of their hunting knives so they could shove them in the muzzles of their rifles and use them as bayonets. He led charge after charge at the Whig riflemen, who flitted from tree to tree, whether retreating or advancing. A rifle ball ended his career, and the remnants of his command surrendered.

"Bloody Ban" Tarleton, the other spectacular British anti-guerrilla, managed to survive the war, but his "British Legion" (which contained hardly any British but himself and George Hanger) was destroyed along with other British units at the Battle of the Cowpens. Cowpens was Daniel Morgan's last battle and his tactical masterpiece.

Morgan had a mixed army—Continental infantry, state infantry, militia musketeers, militia riflemen, and Continental cavalry—and he used mixed tactics. One of his big worries was that the militia riflemen might decide to go home at the wrong moment. Lord Charles Cornwallis, the British commander in the South, had given Tarleton almost all of his light troops and sent him after Morgan.

Morgan waited for him at the Cowpens, a broad pasture where drovers used to keep their cattle before selling them in the cities. He stationed 120 rifle-armed skirmishers in front of his other troops. Behind them were the militia riflemen, then the Continentals and other musket-armed infantry. Behind them was the Continental cavalry under William Washington, the commander-in-chief's cousin. In back of the cavalry were the riflemen's horses. And behind everything else was the Broad River, a stream that lived up to its name. The militia riflemen were not likely to run away. Morgan asked the skirmishers to aim carefully and withdraw slowly, firing as they withdrew. He asked the line of riflemen behind them to fire two well-aimed shots before they withdrew. The riflemen would pass through the lines of regular infantry and form a new line behind them.

Tarleton considered using his cavalry to sweep around the American flanks, but he could not, because the ground was not suitable for cavalry, and Morgan had stationed flank guards who took advantage of the ample cover in those areas.

The British attacked the skirmisher riflemen with a cavalry charge. Not a good idea, the horsemen decided after seeing their comrades shot out of their saddles. They turned and galloped back to their own lines. The British infantry advanced and fired two volleys, but most of their bullets flew over the heads of the Americans. The American riflemen each picked their own targets and fired. Some of them managed to get off as many as five shots before retiring. British officers and sergeants fell all along the line. The American musket men fired. Their volley was more effective than the British volley had been. Two more American volleys followed. At this point, according to Lieutenant Roderick MacKenzie, a British officer, between a third and a half of the British infantry were down.

When an American unit changed position, the British 71st Highlanders (the Black Watch) thought they were retreating. With a shout of joy, they ran forward, a disorganized mob. The Americans turned and fired a volley. Other American units fired more volleys. The shocked Highlanders surrendered.

Tarleton now sent his cavalry against both American flanks. Washington had about the same number of horsemen, but he did not divide them. He struck each British cavalry unit in turn. He drove one off the field and then the second. The whole British force began a panic-stricken flight.

Tarleton had been so eager to get Morgan he drove his men at top speed, not even stopping to eat on the last day of his march. Morgan used his riflemen, firing from the prone position far beyond the range of British muskets, to break up British cohesion and damage their leadership. As they pushed on, the British encountered successive lines of resistance and finally broke psychologically.

So, the idea that the Americans in the Revolution seldom fought from cover is refuted by the testimony of George Washington and the tactics of riflemen at the battles of Bennington, Saratoga, and Cowpens.

The American Civil War Saw the First Use of Submarines

This is a myth believed by people who have an interest in military history. The average person who cares little for wars of long ago probably thinks submarines first appeared in World War I. Their activities were, of course, the reason the United States got into that war.

In the Civil War, both the Union and the Confederacy did use submarines. Most of them were used to lay mines (or torpedoes, as they were called in those days). One sub, the CSS *Hunley*, sank a warship, the USS *Housatonic*, using a "spar torpedo," an explosive on the end of a long pole. But even then submarines were hardly a new idea. Inventors had been toying with the idea for centuries. Robert Fulton, the steam ship inventor, offered to build one for Napoleon. The Emperor was interested, and Fulton built a sub called *Nautilus* (a name later picked up by Jules Verne for his fictional submarine in *Twenty Thousand Leagues Under the Sea*). At

A German submarine surfaces during World War I.

German submarine warfare brought the United States into World War I. Americans used subs during the American Civil War, but the first use of them in warfare was during the Revolutionary War, when Tuttle's *American Turle* failed to sink a British frigate.

the last minute Napoleon dropped the idea. He did not think using submarines was quite sporting. The French Emperor, although supremely gifted in military strategy and tactics, had little faith in new military ideas. France had been a pioneer in the development of balloons, but Napoleon got rid of his country's balloon fleet. Fulton's submarine would probably have been successful. His collaborator was David Bushnell, who had built the first submarine used in combat.

Bushnell's craft was called *American Turtle*. It went into action on September 6, 1776, in an attempt to sink the frigate HMS *Eagle* in New York harbor. The *Turtle* was a strange-looking craft. It consisted of two solid, curved pieces of wood, carefully fitted together and sealed against leakage. It had room for one man, who entered through a hatch at the top. It had a rudder for steering and a hand-cranked propeller. Its armament was a bomb attached to the front of the sub and to an augur that could be cranked from inside the submarine. In operation, it was to approach the *Eagle* with the hatch open and barely above the water. There was no oxygen supply inside the *Turtle*, so the hatch had to be open most of the time. The hatch was so small, however, that it was most unlikely that anyone would see it at night. When the *Turtle* was close to her target, the operator could close the hatch and use a propeller on the top of the craft to dive below the surface. The sub would drive its auger into the target ship's hull, then release the bomb from the submarine, leaving it still attached to the augur. The *Turtle* would then move away as quickly as possible, surfacing and opening the hatch. The bomb, which had a clockwork delay mechanism, would explode when the submarine was at a safe distance.

Bushnell, a captain in the Continental Army, tested his submarine exhaustively on the Connecticut River before bringing it to New York. His brother, Ezra, was to pilot it against the British flagship, the *Eagle*. The *Turtle* was unlike anything in the water, so Ezra had to practice extensively. Then Bushnell had his first stroke of bad luck. Ezra became violently ill the night before the attack. Another man, Ezra Lee, who had much less experience operating the *American Turtle*, volunteered to take Ezra Bushnell's place.

Lee squeezed through the tiny hatch and moved slowly toward the British ship. He dived at the proper time and put the augur against the *Eagle's* hull. Then came the second stroke of bad luck. The British warship had a copper sheath below the waterline to counter barnacles. The augur couldn't penetrate the sheath. The weight of the submarine was insignificant compared to the frigate, and the hand-cranked propeller gave the submarine little power—not nearly enough to force the augur bit through the copper. Lee tried again without success. Then he became acutely aware of the third bit of bad luck.

The bomb's clockwork detonator, devised by Bushnell and his friends on the scientific faculty of Yale University, had been set before the sub was launched. Lee had no way to stop the ticking. He abandoned the augur with the attached bomb and headed back to shore.

The bomb exploded and the British sailors woke up. They hoisted their sails and moved out of the harbor, not knowing what kind of attack the rebels were making. Bushnell and his people loaded the submarine on a wagon and took it back to New England.

Centuries later, a television crew built a replica of Bushnell's submarine and used it in a documentary. A British television reviewer for the English newspaper *The Telegraph* denounced the show as a hoax, saying Bushnell's claim to have invented a submarine was mere propaganda. Inasmuch as the whole operation was top secret, with no word of it until after the war, it's hard to see how it could have been propaganda. At any rate, at least two replicas of the *American Turtle* have been built, and both of them worked.

After the war, Bushnell petitioned Congress for some sort of recognition. George Washington praised Bushnell and his invention, although bad luck prevented it from accomplishing anything. Congress, though, did nothing. Bushnell went to France, where he joined Robert Fulton in building the submarine Napoleon had rejected. Bitterly disappointed, he returned to the United States, changed his name to Bush, and moved far from Connecticut. It wasn't until 1824 that the people of Warrentown, Georgia, learned that Dr. Bush, who taught science and religion at the local high school, was really David Bushnell, the Revolutionary inventor.

MYTH #13

The British Band Played "The World Turned Upside Down" at Yorktown

Ask any high school student about the surrender of the British at Yorktown, and he or she can tell you that Cornwallis's people marched out silently while their band played a solemn tune called "The World Turned Upside Down." There have been quite a few songs titled "The World Turned Upside Down" or that use that phrase. They range from one written in 1646 to protest the policies of Oliver Cromwell to later ones written to entertain music hall audiences.

In Kenneth Roberts's *Rabble in Arms*, he gives the lyrics to a music hall song with the refrain, "The world turned upside down," which is anything but solemn. It's a comic music hall song in which the singer tells of his success with the fair sex until "I married me a wife, and the world turned upside down." Roberts was a historical novelist renowned for his research, so the song he says was played at the surrender was probably the most popular song in both Britain and America. But in the book, he has the British band play that when Burgoyne surrendered after the Battle of Saratoga, in 1777—four years before Cornwallis surrendered.

Actually, there's no record of what the British bands played at *either* surrender. The parade of the losing armies took so long that the bands had time to play many songs. This brings us to the quaint ceremonies that marked formal surrenders in the 18th century.

British troops surrender at Trenton.
That during the final surrender at Yorktown the British band played "The World Turned Upside Down" is a well-established myth.

If an enemy had fought bravely before being overwhelmed, it was customary for the victor to grant the vanquished the "honors of war." In that case the vanquished army marched out with their muskets on their shoulders, with their flags flying and with their bands playing their enemies' songs. The vanquished troops would then stack their arms and become prisoners of war. For ordinary troops this could mean confinement in, at worst, the infamous prison hulks. For officers, imprisonment was far more comfortable. Officers were often "paroled" (enlisted personnel less so). This meant they were released upon a promise to refrain from further participation in the war. Enemy prisoners could also be "exchanged" on the release of prisoners by the other side. Paroled prisoners could also be exchanged, even if they were living at home. In that case, they were free to rejoin their military forces and continue fighting. After the capture of Charleston, Sir Henry Clinton paroled the rebel militia. Soon afterwards, he revoked the parole and declared that the former rebels were now eligible to be drafted into the King's forces. That was considered a major war crime by the rebels.

If the vanquished were not given the honors of war, they grounded their arms in their own camp or fort and marched out unarmed with their colors cased. Their band played not the victors' music but the songs of their own country.

When General Benjamin Lincoln surrendered Charleston to the British under Sir Henry Clinton, Clinton, out of sheer churlishness, did not grant him the honors of war. So the next year, when Cornwallis surrendered, he did not get the honors of war either.

The humiliation of being beaten and denied the honors of war was so great that Cornwallis pleaded illness and did not come out to surrender. Instead, he sent out his second-in-command, General Charles O'Hara. O'Hara attempted to give his sword to General Jean Baptiste de Rochambeau, but the French officer said George Washington was in command. O'Hara went to Washington, but the American general refused to take the sword of a subordinate and sent O'Hara to Benjamin Lincoln, who had been exchanged after his surrender of Charleston, and was now second in command.

When the British marched out of Yorktown, their band played only British songs.

But what they were, we don't know. The first mention of "The World Turned Upside Down" appeared in 1822, 41 years after the surrender, in volume II of *Anecdotes of the American Revolution* by Alexander Garden.[1]

The British playing "The World Turned Upside Down" makes a good story, but it probably never happened.

MYTH #14

Union Troops Always Outnumbered the Confederates

According to historian Fletcher Pratt, many people in the South believe that the Union forces always outnumbered the Confederates three to one. That belief, he said, is as sacred to them as the Holy Trinity.[1] There's some basis for it too.

The white population of the seceding states was 5.5 million. The population of the free states was 18.9 million.[2] When you deduct the black population of the free states—because the war was well under way before black men could enlist—the free states have a little more than a 3-to-1 advantage.

The Union Army enlisted a total of 2,489,836 white men from the start of the war to its finish. Later in the war, it enlisted another 178,975 black men. It also enlisted 3,530 Native Americans. That's a total of 2,672,341.[3] There were never that many men at any one time. Soldiers die, and in the Civil War, proportionately

A 19th-century engraving of a Union soldier.

by far our bloodiest war, an awful lot of them did. A lot of soldiers on both sides also deserted. Some of them also enlisted several times to collect enlistment bonuses or to get payment from some people who would hire substitutes to avoid the draft.

Estimating the size of the Confederate Army is even harder, because the Confederacy kept no records. Estimates of Confederate enlistments run from 600,000 to 1,400,000. A common estimate of Confederate enlistees is around 750,000. That would still give the Union a little better than a three-to-one advantage.

The Union did have more men under arms than the Confederacy, because it was much more populous. However, there were a lot of slaves in the Confederacy, even though only three fifths of them were counted as part of the population in determining representation in Congress, and for most other records they were simply ignored. There were enough of them to keep the Southern states running while most of the free men were fighting.

In most of the major battles in the Civil War, the Union forces had a numerical advantage, but it seldom approached the mystical three-to-one margin. At Antietam, for instance, McClellan had 84,000 and Lee had 65,000 (although

McClellan thought Lee had 110,000).[4] At Gettysburg, Meade had 88,000 and Lee had 75,000.[5] In neither case was there anything like a three-to-one or even a two-to-one ratio.

Unreconstructed believers in the Northern states' three-to-one numerical superiority ignore one of the Confederacy's most talented general's prescription for victory: "Get there first with the most," said General Nathan B. Forrest.[6] Forrest frequently won his battles, so he must have gotten there with the most several times.

In war, numbers are important, but not all-important. Both sides in the Battle of Chickamauga Creek proved that. The battle occurred at an unhappy time for the Confederacy. Grant had taken Vicksburg, giving the Union control of the Mississippi and effectively cutting the Confederacy in two. At about the same time, Meade, at Gettysburg, had turned back Lee's second invasion of the North.

The effects of both battles, though, have often been exaggerated. There had been very little commerce between the eastern and western sections of the Confederacy. The population of the eastern section was vastly larger and most of the ports and almost all of the factories were in the East. Although it's been called a decisive battle, Gettysburg was no more decisive than Antietam Creek. Both simply proved that Lee could not conquer the North—but he never attempted to do that. What may be considered a more decisive battle was shaping up in neither the East nor the West: A Union army led by William Rosecrans was pushing towards Chattanooga. Facing that was a slightly smaller Confederate army led by Braxton Bragg.

Bragg had a serious weakness for a general: he loved his soldiers and hated to see them die. He once broke down and wept at the thought of leaving a hospital full of wounded men to the advancing Yankees. That weakness made him cautious.

He retreated before Rosecrans, hoping to draw him into a trap. The retreat made Bragg enormously unpopular, especially with Southern newspapers. He was denounced as betraying Southern Honor. Bragg didn't care. He was a soldier, not a politician.

William Rosecrans was also a soldier, and a good one. He feinted at trying to turn Bragg's right flank by marching through the "impassable" pine barrens to his east. Bragg was not deceived. He repulsed Rosecrans's attack near Shelbyville. Fifteen days later, Yankee troops emerged from the pine barrens in Bragg's rear. Rosecrans had feinted not once, but twice— first at the barrens, then at Shelbyville. Then under cover of a blinding rain storm, he marched through the barrens.

Rosecrans feinted again to cross the Tennessee River and get behind Bragg's troops in Chattanooga. Bragg retreated into Georgia and arranged for Robert E. Lee to send him James Longstreet and his corps. In the American Civil War, railroads played an unprecedented role, and reinforcing Bragg was one of their greatest feats. Longstreet's men came from Virginia; troops who escaped the Yankees after the fall of Vicksburg came from Mississippi; a Confederate rear guard arrived from Kentucky. The Yankees were now decisively outnumbered.

Meanwhile, Bragg had recruited volunteers who were both brave and intelligent. They were to allow themselves to be captured by the Yankees and tell them that Bragg's army had been routed and was now an almost leaderless mob running through the mountains. They had to be brave, because in a Civil War prison camp death from starvation or sickness was more likely than death on the battlefield.

Rosecrans's 57,000 troops rushed into the mountains after the supposedly routed enemy. Bragg planned to smite them with reinforced army of 66 to 70 thousand. One Union division, Negley's, was well ahead of Rosecrans's main body. Bragg ordered Leonidas Polk, an Episcopal bishop in civilian life, to send Hindman's division to stop Negley, and he told D.H. Hill (like Longstreet, a veteran of Lee's Army of Northern Virginia) to send up Cleburne's division to finish off the Union troops.

Nothing happened. Bragg ordered Simon Bolivar Buckner to take two divisions of his corps and join Hindman. Then Bragg asked Hill where Cleburne was. Hill said the Irish-born general was sick. Bragg rode to Cleburne's area and found the Irishman perfectly healthy and astounded that anyone had reported him ill. Hindman and Buckner, meanwhile, decided they had a better plan than the commanding general. While they sent back a courier to get approval for their plan, Negley withdrew.

By this time, Rosecrans realized he was not chasing a panic-stricken mob. He ordered his troops to close up their line and guard the road to Chattanooga. Bragg realized he couldn't depend on his subordinates to carry out any complicated maneuvers. His plan of attack was so simple nobody could say he didn't understand it. At dawn, the farthermost right division of his line, one of Polk's corps, would attack. As soon as it heard gunfire, the division to the left of that would attack, then the division just left of that, and so on. A lot of soldiers died, but the attack was making no progress.

"Old Pete" Longstreet was no genius, but he wasn't an idiot either. He knew that this idiotic plan would soon erase Bragg's numerical advantage. He formed his divisions into a long column. They would concentrate on one spot in the Union line and break through.

Just before it was Longstreet's turn to attack, a Union staff officer riding behind the line passed the spot held by Brannan's division. The division was in the woods and he couldn't see them. When he reached Rosecrans's headquarters, he reported that there was a gap in the line south of Reynolds's division. Rosecrans, busy trying to direct a battle, said, without thinking much about it, "Tell General Wood to close that gap."[7]

Wood obeyed the order, and that left a real gap in the Union line—directly across from Longstreet's division. Longstreet's men poured through the gap, and Rosecrans's whole right wing melted away.

Rosecrans followed the right wing and tried to reorganize them. His chief of staff, James A. Garfield, told Rosecrans his place was here with the bulk of the army to prevent a rout. He, Garfield, would join the left wing, under George Thomas, a Virginian who refused to join the secessionists, to ensure that whatever Thomas needed would be delivered. (After the war, Garfield was elected president, partially because he claimed that he had stayed with Thomas at Chickamauga when the commanding general ran away.) Meanwhile, Thomas, with less than half of the originally outnumbered army, repulsed attack after attack. His men were running out of ammunition.

"Fix bayonets," said "Old Pap" Thomas. His men repulsed the next attack, many of them with cold steel. As it grew dark, Longstreet asked Bragg to send him men from Polk's corps. He was told that Polk had lost so many men that none were available. After nightfall, Thomas marched his men back to Chattanooga in good order.

The Confederate troops had every advantage—surprise, position, and overwhelming numbers—but they couldn't crush Thomas's corps. Technically, they had won a victory. How much they had lost did not become apparent until later.

Bragg laid siege to Chattanooga. Grant and his army came down from Vicksburg to break the siege. He sent a convoy of supplies over the mountains to the garrison of Chattanooga. Confederate besiegers tried to stop it, but they were routed—not by Union infantry but by some frightened, stampeding mules. After that, they made no attempt to close the "cracker line." Bragg contented himself with holding the heights on the south side of the Tennessee River, where his guns could command all approaches to Chattanooga.

Grant decided to break the siege. He sent "Fighting Joe" Hooker and William T. Sherman from his Vicksburg army against the besiegers. Hooker was stopped by a flooded swamp and Sherman by unmapped territory and Pat Cleburne, the Confederacy's best division commander. Thomas, who had replaced Rosecrans, was to make a diversion below Missionary Ridge. Thomas's troops took the outposts at the base of the ridge, then came under fire from the top of the mountain.

Missionary Ridge is a steep, rocky mountain that an unencumbered man, using both hands, can climb in half a day. Some of the troops began to climb. General Philip Sheridan lifted a bottle of whiskey and toasted the defenders on the ridge. They fired a cannon at him.

"I find that damned ungrateful," Sheridan said. "Just for that I'll take that gun." He began climbing and Thomas's whole army joined him. The Confederates on the ridge dropped their rifles, abandoned their cannons, and dashed down the opposite slope. Bragg tried to rally them. They ignored him.

"No satisfactory excuse can possibly be given for the shameful conduct of the troops on the left [of Missionary Ridge] for allowing their line to be penetrated," Bragg reported. "The position was one which ought to have been held with a line of skirmishers against an assaulting column."[8]

D.H. Hill had one explanation: "After Chickamauga, the *élan* of the Southern soldier was never seen again."[9]

Years later, at a reunion of Chickamauga veterans, a Confederate veteran talking to a Union veteran had an earthier explanation: "You Yanks got into our inwards."

Myth #15

The Only Aircraft in the Civil War Were Tethered Balloons

Almost everybody knows that the Civil War was the first American war that used aircraft. And everybody knows too that those aircraft were balloons tied to the ground.

On July 18, 1861, Thaddeus Sobieski Constantine Lowe commanded the balloon *Enterprise* while a telegraph operator sent history's first air-to-ground message. Three and a half months later, Lowe was promoted to "Chief Astronaut" of the Army of the Potomac's new "Balloon Corps." The seven balloons in the corps were a great help—their observers could locate enemy positions, see where artillery shells were striking, and report what they saw to the ground. They were usually tied to the ground, but during General George B. McClellan's Peninsular Campaign, they were tethered to a coal barge moving on the river to keep pace with the army.

Balloon Corps Transport, with Lord R...berts' Army—advance on Johannesburg, S. A.
Copyright 1900 by Underwood & Underwood.

Tethered balloons like this one were the only official
aircraft in the Civil War, but the Union missed a
chance to get a far more formidable aircraft.

These Civil War balloons are well known. Most people, in
fact, think they were the *only* aircraft in existence during the
Civil War. The truth is that tethered balloons were just the
only aircraft *used* in the Civil War. There was another aircraft,
though: a swift-moving, maneuverable dirigible that was offered to the government but rejected. Details about the airship
and the reason for its rejection are both mysterious, and all
of the mystery has not been solved in a century and a half.
But there is no doubt that it worked; its flights were witnessed
and described in newspapers. After the war, it even carried
passengers.

Outwardly, there was nothing mysterious about Dr.
Solomon Andrews of Perth Amboy, New Jersey, the inventor of the aircraft. He was the son of a Presbyterian minister
and a practicing physician with an interest in engineering. He
was also quite successful. He served three terms as mayor of
Perth Amboy and had been Port Collector of Perth Amboy
and president of the city's Board of Health. He built the

first sewer in Perth Amboy and was credited with saving his hometown from cholera and yellow fever epidemics. On the side, Andrews invented things. His 24 successful inventions included a sewing machine, a kitchen range, a barrel-making machine, a gas lamp, and a padlock.

To promote the padlock, he put $1,000 cash in a box, chained the box to a lamp post in downtown New York, and locked it with his padlock. He then announced that anyone who could pick the lock could keep the money. Every crook in New York tried, and they all failed. Sales of the lock brought Dr. Andrews $30,000.

In 1849, he began working on his airship. He later said he made many mistakes, but he learned from them. Using a scale model, he taught himself how to fly the contraption as inconspicuously as possible. In September 5, 1862, he was ready to go public.

He could not have picked a better time. Washington was in a panic. Stonewall Jackson had trounced the Union army at the Second Battle of Bull Run, and Robert E. Lee had begun his first invasion of the North. Confederate gunboats were seen on the Potomac. Andrews told Secretary of War Edwin Stanton that he could build a flying machine that could buck the stiffest wind and fly 10 miles into Confederate territory and back. Stanton sent him to the Bureau of Topographical Engineers to describe his invention.

"What will it cost?" asked a Captain Lee, one of the engineers.

"Not over five thousand dollars, and I'll guarantee its success or no pay."[1]

"What motive power will you use, Dr. Andrews?" another engineer asked.

"Gravitation," Andrews said. He offered no other explanation.

Apparently, the bureau was not convinced. It reported that "the device appears to be ingenious to a high degree but we are not fully convinced of its practical utility."[2]

Unable to convince the engineers of his theory, Andrews went home and built a full-size airship. He called it *Aereon*, meaning the "age of air."

The *Aereon* consisted of three sausage-shaped balloons, each 13 feet in diameter and 80 feet long. Each balloon had seven inner cells to prevent movement of the hydrogen filling. Slung beneath the three balloons was a basket 16 inches wide and 12 feet long. Also beneath the balloons was a "ballast car" on tracks. To dive, the operator moved the ballast forward; to climb, he moved it back. To maneuver laterally, the airship had a rudder.

At the end of May, 1863, Andrews squeezed into the basket and shouted to his ground crew, "Cut loose!"[3]

Solomon Andrews's ungainly looking vehicle rose gracefully to a height of 200 feet. It flew over the field, apparently blown by the wind. Then it turned and flew into the wind. A few minutes later, it glided down to the crew, who held its mooring ropes while Andrews climbed out of the basket.

Andrews made a few more test flights. He decided that the inner cells were unnecessary and took them out. That lightened the ship by 180 pounds. The 17-foot square rudder seemed too sensitive, so he made it smaller. He found, too, that by shifting his weight in the basket, he could change the *Aereon's* vertical direction, so the ballast car was unnecessary.

Word of the strange balloon began to spread in northern New Jersey and New York City. Andrews invited some prominent skeptics to a demonstration of his improved *Aereon*. It climbed high in the sky and flew over the sea, then turned and returned, according to a witness, "faster than a cannon ball."[4]

When Andrews landed, the one-time skeptics cheered.

Andrews planned to convince the War Department by flying the *Aereon* from Perth Amboy to New York. A lawyer friend warned him, however, that even though the airship had been rejected, the dirigible was "contraband of war," and a public flight, unlike the semi-private tests he had made, might give Confederate agents information on how the ship worked.

On August 26, 1863, Andrews wrote to Abraham Lincoln. He said he would make one more test, during which he would drop all the ballast to see how fast his craft would fly. Then he would destroy it so the Confederates would not be able to copy it. He asked the President that he "select some suitable person, the more scientific and practical the better, and send him here that he may examine the machine and witness the trial."[5]

He got no answer.

Andrews decided to hold a test anyhow, without a presidential witness.

Rumors about the strange aircraft were widespread, and a large crowd appeared to witness the flight. Reporters from several New York newspapers were present.

One witness, James Allen, who came to scoff, was shocked when Andrews turned the *Aereon* around. "It's as easy as a steamboat could be turned!" he cried.[6] When Andrews landed, he cut the basket off the balloons and removed all the ballast. Then he lashed the rudder to one side and released his brainchild. The *Aereon* shot up, spiraling in circles about three quarters of a mile in diameter.

A reporter from the New York *Herald* wrote that the craft was traveling at least 120 miles an hour. Of course, nobody in 1863 had ever seen any kind of vehicle travel at 120 miles an hour. Ellis C. Waite, an architect who had helped Andrews, said, "I never saw any vessel, railroad car, or any other thing of magnitude go so fast."[7]

The airship spiraled with the wind and against it. About two miles above the earth, it flew into a mass of clouds and was never seen again.

The New York *Herald* called *Aereon* "the most extraordinary invention of the age," but the Webster, Massachusetts *Times* warned that "with such a machine in the hands of Jefferson Davis, the armies around Washington would be powerless to defend the capital."[8]

Encouraged, Andrews hounded the War Department. He was finally given a personal interview with President Lincoln. He told Lincoln about the last trial. The President asked if there were any witnesses. When Andrews said there were, Lincoln asked him to have "four or five respectable persons write to me and what they saw. Then I will take action on it."[9]

Andrews had five "respectable" witnesses, professionals and public officials, write to the President.

He heard nothing more.

In January 1864, he petitioned the Senate and House of Representatives, and said that if no action were taken, he would fly a new airship over Washington. Finally, he was allowed to give a demonstration before the military committees of the House and Senate. He appeared with a 4-foot rubber model airship. It flew across the room. He set the rudder at an angle and the little dirigible flew in circles. The congressmen asked the Secretary of War to appoint a scientific commission to look into Andrews' invention and make a report.

Andrews was sure his invention would be accepted.

But again, time passed with no word from Washington.

When Andrews investigated, he learned that the letters to Lincoln from his witnesses had been mislaid and never reached the president. And the report of the scientific commission had never reached Secretary of War Stanton. He finally got a letter from a member of the House Military Committee who was interested in the invention, and said that his struggle to have it accepted was "a hopeless effort against doubt and prejudice."[10]

The war was almost over and nobody was interested in Andrews' marvelous invention.

Andrews had more bad luck. He fell from a carriage and broke his arm. While recuperating, he wrote a book called *The Art of Flying*. He maintained that the difference in specific gravity between the balloon and the atmosphere could be used to power the airship in any direction. The trouble was that nobody could understand his theory.

Andrews founded a commercial airship company and planned to make passenger flights between New York and Philadelphia. He built a new airship, one that had only one balloon—a huge, lemon-shaped gas bag that was pointed on each end. He flew over New York City, taking along his two partners in the Aerial Navigation Company, C.M. Plumb and G. Waldo Hill. The flight created a sensation in the city. The *Aereon II* climbed to 6,000 feet and disappeared into the clouds. It came out again, flew over Long Island Sound, and landed in Astoria.

Andrews took Plumb up again on another flight over the city. Once again, he created a sensation and inspired stories in the newspapers. But the Aerial Navigation Company had run out of money, was deeply in debt, and was ignored by investors. Dr. Andrews went back to the practice of medicine and remains the only person in history to pilot a dirigible into the wind without an engine—which he did, we must remember, during the time of the Civil War.

Myth #16

Custer's Stand Was His Last Because the Indians Had Repeaters

This myth has appeared in innumerable movies and television shows. It may be popular because everybody likes to hear about government blunders. For some people, it's an article of faith that private enterprise can do anything and everything more efficiently than government. In truth, there were plenty of repeating rifles around when Custer and his men rode out to the Little Bighorn River, but they were made for sale to hunters and other individuals who had a need for a rifle. Federal troops didn't carry them.

There were a couple of serious errors concerning weapons, but the War Department didn't make them. Custer's superior officer, Gen. Alfred Terry, made one of them. Custer himself made an even more serious one. But the biggest factor in the defeat was the fearlessness—not bravery but fearlessness—of George Armstrong Custer.

But first, let's consider rifles, both single shots and repeaters.

A couple of repeating rifles had been used in significant numbers during the Civil War: the Spencer and the Henry. The Henry, a lever-action rifle, was invented by B. Tyler Henry, who founded a company that was later purchased by Oliver Winchester. In his design, a tubular magazine beneath the barrel could be loaded with 12 cartridges. With one cartridge in the chamber, the Henry was a 13-shot repeater. The trigger guard was a lever that could be pulled down to both cock the hammer and reload the chamber. According to legend, the Confederates called the Henry "that damned Yankee rifle they load on Sunday and fire all week." The other repeater was the Spencer, an invention of Christopher Spencer, who got his rifle accepted for service by demonstrating it to President Lincoln himself. Pulling down the trigger guard similarly reloaded the Spencer's chamber, but the firer had to cock the hammer separately. The Spencer's seven-round magazine in the rifle's stock could be loaded much faster than the Henry's magazine.

Both rifles were extremely deadly at close quarters. At the Battle of Chickamauga, a column of Confederates charging Wilder's Lightning Brigade seemed to rush forward to a certain point and then drop into a hole in the ground when hit by the continuous fire of the Spencers.

The trouble with the repeaters was that the cartridges were generally much less powerful than those of the single-shot rifles like the Sharps, or even the old muzzle-loaders. In Custer's time the repeaters used cartridges like the .44-40 and .38-40, which in modern times have been used only in revolvers and are now obsolete—no guns at all are being made for them.

The War Department, stuck with a huge number of muzzle-loaders after the Civil War, turned these into breech-loaders using the invention of E.S. Allin, master armorer of the Springfield Armory. Allin added a hinged breechblock that opened upward to the end of the barrel of the former muzzle-loaders. The lock wasn't as strong as those of contemporary breech-loaders like the Remington, Sharps, or Peabody, but it was perfectly adequate for the black powder cartridges of the time.

It was so adequate, in fact, that the next two standard rifles adopted were *made with* Allin's "trapdoor" action. They used two new cartridges, the .50-70 and the .45-70.

The .45-70 cartridge, unlike the early repeater cartridges, is still being made, and rifles chambered for it are also still being made. It is powerful enough to stop any animal in North America, and, if the shooter is a good judge of distance, is accurate at more than a mile. The .45-70 Springfield was made in both rifle and carbine (a short barrel rifle) versions. Custer's cavalrymen carried the carbine, which was easier to use on horseback.

So did any Native American who could get hold of one. Geronimo, the famous Apache chief, is holding a .45-70 carbine in almost all of his photos.

But only some of the Indians at the Little Bighorn had rifles of any kind. Their main missile weapon was the bow and arrow, and the Native Americans did things with this ancient device you couldn't do with a rifle: At one point in the battle, they crouched below a hill where the troopers couldn't see them and shot their arrows high in the air. The arrows fell almost straight down on Custer's men. The archers of William the Conqueror used this tactic in 1066. It still worked. For close-quarters fighting, the Native Americans had clubs and hatchets.

And that brings us to the error of General Terry. He ordered Custer to leave all his regiment's sabers at their base. Sabers, he believed, were only an encumbrance in "Indian" fighting; you never got close enough to use a saber. He couldn't imagine that the "Indians" would overrun a U.S. Army unit and finish it off with clubs and hatchets. In a fight between a man with a club or hatchet and one with a sword, always put your money on the swordsman—provided he *has* his sword.

Terry could have made up for that error if Custer had taken his further advice. Terry suggested that the cavalrymen take along three Gatling guns. The Gatling was a hand-operated machine gun. It had a bundle of barrels (10 or six was the usual number) that revolved as a gunner turned a crank. At different points in the rotation, a barrel was loaded, fired, and the empty shell ejected. A strong gunner could fire at the rate of a thousand shots a minute. If the Seventh Cavalry had its Gatling guns, it's doubtful that the Native Americans could ever have gotten close enough to use clubs and hatchets. But Custer didn't take them because he thought they would be an encumbrance. He hated encumbrances; anything that would slow his progress. The Gatlings, though, were not the kind that had to be towed on a wheeled carriage; they were designed to be disassembled and carried on pack mules. Evan Connell, in *Son of the Morning Star*, says of the Gatlings, "They frequently malfunctioned, and the bullets they sprayed from six or 10 barrels—depending on the model—would have been effective only against a mass attack, such as might have been expected in Europe. British redcoats might march into the fire of Gatlings with heads up and arms swinging, but American Indians were less disciplined."[1]

The Gatling gun, the first successful machine gun. Although it required a gunner to crank it, the Gatling was a most formidable weapon and was the reason that Custer's Last Stand near the Little Bighorn was, in fact, his last.

Three years after Custer decided not to use the three Gatling guns, the British took two Gatlings to Zululand in South Africa. The Zulus were the most militarily sophisticated people in Africa and masters of cover and concealment. They had annihilated a British army many times the size of Custer's force. But the British Gatlings mowed them down and ended the Zulu War.

The big problem, though, was not what weapons the Native Americans had or Custer lacked. It was Custer himself. He had graduated near the bottom of his class at West Point, but had risen like a rocket during the Civil War. He always volunteered to scout enemy positions where everyone else feared to go. He reported what he saw accurately, because no enemy could spook him. He led charges no matter how the odds looked. At Gettysburg, commanding a Michigan volunteer brigade, he drove J.E.B. Stuart's supposedly invincible Confederate cavalry from the field. And unlike some commanders, he *led* his men. He didn't push them. No one could dispute his bravery. But at the Little Bighorn, he revealed another element of his character. When Custer saw the Native American camp—containing from 3,000 to 5,000 warriors, the largest concentration of Native American fighting men north of the Rio Grande in history—and many more women and children, his only concern was to attack them before they could get away. He had been ordered to wait for two other units, one led by General Terry and the other by Colonel John Gibbon, which were converging on the Native Americans from different directions. Already outnumbered at least 5 to 1, Custer sent a quarter of his force off to look for Native Americans who might be hiding in the waterless badlands to the south of the encampment. He sent couriers to gather other scattered units, but he attacked before they arrived. He had, in effect, abandoned seven of his 12 companies and was moving against 3,000 to 5,000 warriors with about 300 troopers.

The only explanation for Custer's actions was that he was quite literally fearless. A brave person recognizes danger, but performs in spite of it. But anyone ignoring the odds Custer faced would have to be irrationally without a healthy amount of fear—especially when reinforcements were coming who would even the odds.

The fact that Custer lost had nothing to do with the Native Americans having repeating rifles. They may have had a few, but with the odds they had in their favor, they would have wiped out Custer's troops even if they didn't have a single gun.

MYTH #17

Latin American Warfare Was Never Serious

For some reason, Americans for many years had the idea that warfare in Latin America consisted of revolutions fought by armies mainly composed of generals and colonels—wars that produced many changes of government but few casualties. Lately, our perception has changed; we know that there have been and are many serious matters in Latin America—massacres, death squads, terrorists, and so on. But serious warfare between sovereign states? That doesn't happen. We think.

This demonstrates one of the great gaps in our educational system: Most reasonably well-read people know something about the Hundred Years' War between England and France, the Eighty Years' War between Spain and the Netherlands, the Thirty Years' War with most of Europe participating in a German civil war. They've heard of the Boer War in Africa and various wars of conquest by Britain, France, Belgium, Germany, and Spain in Africa. But the southern part of North America and all of South America is a historical terra incognita.

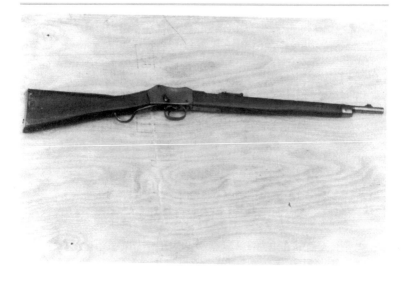

**A British Martini-Henry carbine. British weapons were
common during the War of the Triple Alliance.**

No Latin American war is more unknown than the War
of the Triple Alliance in 1865–70. Yet this totally ignored war,
of Paraguay versus Argentina, Brazil, and Uruguay, is, proportionately, one of the bloodiest in history—for South America
or anywhere else. Paraguay began the war. By the time it ended,
Paraguay's population, according to one reliable estimate, had
dropped from 1,337,000 to 220,000.[1] At the end of the war,
the Paraguayan army consisted mostly of 12-year-old boys.
The adult male population of Paraguay had been virtually
annihilated.

Here's what happened.

Paraguay had an unusual colonial history. The country
had been inhabited by the very peaceful Guaraní Indians.
Jesuit missionaries arrived in the late 1500s and set up a

semi-communistic society among the Guaranís. They forbade Spanish and Portuguese adventurers from entering their territory, because most Europeans came to Guaraní country to capture slaves. The Indians led regimented but apparently happy lives. They mourned the Jesuits when, after complaints by Spanish settlers that the missionaries were preventing them from exploiting the land (and its people), the king of Spain in 1767 expelled the Jesuits from all Spanish territory.

The Guaranís gave the king no trouble, and their swampy land attracted few Europeans. But in the early 19th century, revolution, inspired by the French Revolution, which had been inspired by the United States Revolution, was in the air. In 1811, after the people of Buenos Aires declared their independence from Spain, Paraguay followed suit. A short time later, Dr. José Rodríguez de Francia y Velasco made himself dictator. Francia was one of the only two Paraguayans with a doctorate. His was in theology. He had been training to enter the Catholic priesthood, but he found running a country a more satisfying career. He was one of a class that Latinos call *"caudillos bárbaros."* Paraguay has had far more than its share of such leaders.

Francia tried to keep Paraguay as isolated as it had been under the Jesuits, but he was no Jesuit: He seized all the property of the Catholic Church and appointed himself head of the Church. He discouraged weddings, and insisted that he personally officiate at every wedding in the country. Everyone had to raise his hat when he passed, and those without hats had to carry a hat brim to raise. He established a secret police corps to enforce his decrees and executed hordes of people. He was probably mad, but the Paraguayans put up with him.

When Francia died, he was succeeded by a new caudillo bárbaro, Carlos Antonio López. López continued two of Francia's policies: striving to make Paraguay completely self-sufficient and brooking no dissent from the president's rule. Francia had no legitimate children, but Carlos López did, and he intended to start a dynasty. He made his son, Francisco Solano López, a brigadier general at the age of 18, and nine years later, in 1853, sent him to Britain, France, and Italy as minister plenipotentiary to purchase weapons, ships, and military supplies.

Francisco López greatly admired the empire of Napoleon III and Napoleon's army. He also admired a young Irish woman named Eliza Lynch. Eliza Lynch (or Elisa, the Spanish spelling she adopted) was born in Cork, Ireland, but she had married a French officer at the age of 15. They were soon divorced, and Eliza took up with a Russian nobleman. When the Crimean War broke out, the Russian went home and left her in Paris. She was a strikingly beautiful 18-year-old when Lopez met her. He was a short, dumpy man of 27 who always wore a military uniform weighed down with medals. Most Parisians considered him a fool, but Eliza Lynch thought he had possibilities. She became his mistress and stayed with him when he returned to Paraguay.

When he returned, Carlos Antonio López appointed him minister of war and then vice president. When the elder López died, Francisco Solano López became president.

At this time, the Rio de la Plata states (Argentina, Brazil, Paraguay, and Uruguay) were a restless area. In most of Latin America at this time, there were two political parties: the Blancos (Whites) and the Colorados (Reds). Members of these parties frequently felt more loyalty their party in other countries than they did to the other party in their own country. Brazil was the largest and most powerful state. It was also an empire, ruled at this time by Emperor Dom Pedro II. Next to the United States in North America, it was the largest slave-owning nation in the world. Argentina was the second power of South America, and a republic, lately free of one of the most barbarous of the caudillos bárbaros, Juan Manuel de Rosas. Argentina and Brazil were serious rivals, and each had its eyes on Paraguay. Uruguay was a gaucho republic, an area of near-anarchy masquerading as a nation.

Brazil had several times intervened in the internal affairs of Uruguay. In 1864, Dom Pedro claimed that Brazilian citizens were being robbed by Uruguayans, which was probably true, and the Uruguayan government did nothing about it. Uruguay at the time was controlled by the Colorado Party. Bartolome Mitre, president of Argentina, was a Blanco. He was not opposed to Brazil's invasion; Francisco Solano López was his own party. He saw Brazil's action as a large nation bullying a small one.

López's nation, like Uruguay, was a small one, sandwiched between the two largest countries in South America. But unlike Uruguay, Paraguay was not defenseless. Although landlocked, it had, for South America, a reasonably strong navy. And, thanks to Francisco Solano López and his father, the largest army in South America. The army contained at least 70,000 men, but it lacked a reliable source of military supplies and reserves.[2] It also lacked an efficient chain of command. Junior officers had neither experience nor authority: all orders had to come from López. There was no military power in South America that compared with the United States, which in 1865 had the largest army and navy in the world.

López reacted to Brazil's invasion of Uruguay by seizing a Brazilian ship. Captured with the ship was the governor of Brazil's Mato Grosso Province. López then, in March 1865, launched part of his army north into Mato Grosso. Some of the Paraguayans pushed into the Brazilian province of Rio Grande do Sul. Mato Grosso was a wild area whose name means "great hunting ground"—it was not an area López coveted, and it was not where the Brazilian Army was. The northward Paraguayan move was a diversion. The bulk of the Brazilian troops were in Uruguay, south of Paraguay. Paraguay did not border Uruguay. The best way to Uruguay from Paraguay was through Argentina. López asked Argentina for permission to send troops through its territory to get to Uruguay. López didn't know Argentina had approved the Brazilian move. He may have counted on Argentina's traditional rivalry with Brazil, but Paraguay was not one of Brazil's favorite countries either. Brazil had had a number of border skirmishes with the Paraguayans during the reign of Carlos Antonio López, and Bartolome Mitre, the president of Argentina, was a Blanco, the party Brazil had restored to power after the invasion. Argentina refused permission.

López didn't care. He sent troops into Argentina. Then, Argentina, Brazil, and the new Blanco government of Uruguay signed a treaty and declared war on Paraguay on May 1, 1865, which became the War of the Triple Alliance.

All three allies began major recruiting drives. Little Uruguay raised around 40,000 troops; Argentina contributed an estimated 100,000, including Bartolome Mitre, the first commanding general of the allied force. But as it turned out, Mitre did not add much strength to the allies. Brazil called up its National Guard, created a Volunteer force (as the United States had done a few years earlier in its Civil War), and freed slaves who would fight in the war. A large portion of the Brazilian army were slaves or free blacks. Brazil's army during the war was estimated to include 150,000 men. Its most formidable force, though, was its navy, which had 42 ships, some of them ironclads.

Before long, the allied troops outnumbered Paraguay's 10 to 1.

López's navy supported the invasion of Argentina and blockaded the Argentine port of Corrientes while the Paraguayans took Corrientes City. Brazil sent troops into Mato Grosso, but they didn't find any Paraguayans. They decided to invade Paraguay, but the Paraguayan cavalry drove them out. The Paraguayans held a portion of Mato Grosso until 1868, when they were shifted to the southern front.

By that time, the outcome of the war had already been decided. On July 11, 1865, at the Battle of Riachuelo, the Brazilian ironclads and other ships had wiped out the Paraguayan Navy. The roads in the Rio de la Plata Basin were few and terrible; all travel was by river craft. The troops in Argentina were cut off, and allied ships blocked any supplies Lopez might get from the outside world. By the end of 1865, the Triple Alliance had taken the offensive.

On September 12, 1866, López asked Mitre to discuss peace terms. Mitre said Paraguay would have to accept every condition specified in the Secret Treaty of the Triple Alliance, one of which called for the war to continue until the current government of Paraguay ceased to be—in other words, the death of Francisco Solano López.

The Paraguayans fought on. Toward the end of the war, many of them had no weapons but machetes and lances. López designated one man in each squad to kill any of his fellow soldiers who showed signs that he might surrender. Eliza Lynch organized Paraguayan women into a cavalry brigade and led charges on horseback. If any man deserted, she or López would flog his wife to death. López became paranoid and executed hundreds he suspected of defeatism—including two of his brothers and two of his brothers-in-law. To save ammunition, executions were carried out by a lance thrust.

On the Allied side, Mitre had repeatedly failed to take fortified Paraguayan positions and thus was replaced by the Brazilian
Marquis of Caxias. Caxias bypassed the forts and laid siege to
the Paraguayan stronghold of Humaita. When Humaita finally
fell, Caxias slipped through the swamps and jungle and attacked Lopez's army from behind. On January 5, 1869, Caxias
entered Asunción, the Paraguayan capital. Francisco Solano
Lopez fled to the mountains north of Asuncion.

Troops of the Triple Alliance began raiding Paraguayan vil-
lages and killing any men who looked capable of bearing arms.
Sometimes they killed the women and children too. But the
Paraguayans fought on.

On March 1, 1870, Brazilian cavalry surprised López, who
was accompanied by 200 soldiers. There are many stories about
the end of Francisco Solano López. One, popular in Argentina,
is that a Brazilian cavalryman named Cabo ("corporal" in
English) Chico Diablo (an improbable name, but he may have
been a slave) picked out López because he was the only fat man
in this camp of starving people, and ran him through with his
lance. An Argentine wit made up a rhyme:

Cabo Chico Diablo	Corporal Chico Diablo
Cabó el diablo chico	Put an end to the young devil

Eliza Lynch was deported to France, where she eventually
died in poverty.

The Argentine death toll has been estimated at 10,000, as
has that of Uruguay, and the Brazilian death toll at 100,000.[3]

The war had some good effects: It is credited with beginning the abolition of slavery in Brazil and with uniting war-
lord-plagued Argentina.

The war brought no benefit to Paraguay. It lost large chunks of territory to Argentina and Brazil. Brazil occupied the country for six years, ostensibly to preserve law and order, but actually to keep Argentina out. But neither Argentina nor Brazil, after the losses they had suffered in the last war, wanted to fight each other. And the depopulated country made a good buffer between the two major South American powers. The war practically destroyed Paraguay as a nation. It had to endure a long line of caudillos bárbaros, the last of whom was Alfredo Stroessner, who was ousted in 1989.

A poet quoted by John Crow wrote a dirge for Paraguay:

Llora, llora urutaú	Weep, weep urutau bird
en las ramas del yatay;	In the branches of the yatay tree
Ya no existe el Paraguay	Now Paraguay does not exist
donde naci como tu	Where I, like you, was born
Llora, llora urutaú.	Weep, weep urutau bird.[4]

MYTH #18

The .45 Automatic Helped Conquer the Philippines

Everyone with an interest in weapons knows the story: When the United States won the war with Spain and acquired the Philippine Islands, our occupation was opposed by the fanatical Moros, resulting in the Philippine Insurrection. Our service handgun, a .38 caliber revolver, was unable to stop the charges of the savage Moros, who, while full of .38 bullets, chopped up many U.S. officers with their bolos. So we adopted the .45 automatic pistol, which proved to be an excellent Moro stopper and ended the Philippine Insurrection.

The only thing wrong with this story is everything. Just about every detail is untrue. I'll start at the beginning...

There was a Philippine Insurrection, but it was against Spain, not the United States. It began before the Spanish-American War, about the same time that a similar insurrection began in Cuba. It continued while we were fighting Spain, and by the time the Spanish surrendered to us, the Filipinos had pushed the Spanish out of more than 90 percent of the Philippines.

Fighting between the Americans and Filipinos, originally allies, began *before* the treaty with Spain, which would transfer the islands to the United States, was ratified by the Senate. The United States had no legal claim to the islands when the Philippine War began, therefore the fighting was a war, not an insurrection.

The Filipino *Insurrectos*, as the Spanish called them, had adopted a constitution modeled after that of the United States and had elected a president, Emilio Aguinaldo, who became fairly close to Admiral George Dewey, the victor in the Battle of Manila Bay. Dewey led "Don Emilio" to believe there would be an alliance with the United States. American forces didn't do much in the Philippines after the naval battle, and they joined Aguinaldo's army in the siege of Manila. Aguinaldo didn't know it, but the American troops in the Philippines had been told that they were an army of occupation, not Philippine allies—so they acted like occupiers, not allies.

The occupying troops were mostly country boys from Kansas, Montana, and other western states. They knew almost nothing about the islands before they arrived in Manila—they could not be expected to know anything when most politicians and newspaper publishers didn't know anything either.

Newspapers of the time, both "imperialist" and "anti-imperialist," portrayed the Filipinos as grass-skirted savages. President William McKinley, on November 29, 1898, announced that he was going to annex the islands to "educate the Filipinos, and uplift and civilize and Christianize them."[1]

McKinley was talking about the only Christian nation in the Far East, one that had about the same proportion of Christians in its population as the United States! There were some Muslims (the famous Moros) in the southernmost islands and a few Pagans in the mountains of Luzon, but the

U.S. troops fire on Philippine nationalist forces during the Philippine War of 1989-1902. Despite the widespread legend, the .45 automatic pistol played no part in that war. The pistol was adopted in 1911.

United States had Apaches, Comanches, Lakotas, and other tribesmen as un-Christian and "uncivilized" as any Philippine Igorot.[2] Almost all Filipinos had adopted European civilization 300 year earlier. The "uncivilized" Filipinos included doctors, lawyers (like Aguinaldo), engineers, and other professionals. Manila had electric lights and electric street cars before most U.S. cities.

Although they had been fighting the same enemy, the American troops treated the Filipinos as if they were an enemy population. They called the Filipinos "niggers" and searched their houses and persons without warrants. They knocked down any Filipino who didn't show them "respect," but showed no respect for the Filipina women they searched. "We have to kill one or two [Filipinos] every night," one private wrote home.[3]

On the night of February 4, 1899, 36 hours before the Senate was scheduled to vote on the treaty with Spain, several drunken Filipinos approached an American sentry post. Private William Grayson called, "Halt." One of the Filipino mocked him, calling "Halto."

"Well, I thought the best thing to do was shoot him," Grayson testified later.[4] A second sentry shot a second Filipino, Grayson shot another, and then the shooting became general. The Filipinos, at first just some drunks wandering around, were heavily out-gunned. Some Filipino soldiers who were on duty joined in. And then the warships in the harbor trained their big guns on the Filipino positions.

The next day, Aguinaldo proposed to the American army commander, General Elwell S. Otis, that they establish a neutral zone between their armies. Otis had no wish for peace. "The fighting, having begun, must go on to the grim end," he said.[5]

So much for the notion that our Philippine campaign was an "insurrection." What about those super-tough Moros?

Our opponents in the Philippine War, one that was a lot bloodier than the war with Spain, were almost 100 percent Catholic Christians. We bought off most of the Moros in the southern islands. Eventually, we did have some fights with the Moros, but they were a feeble foe. The Moros were governed by independent chiefs called datus who seldom cooperated with each other. Individual Moros were mighty warriors, but as a people, not at all formidable.

The .38 revolver was far from a satisfactory sidearm, but there are very few cases of a Filipino, hit with a .38 caliber bullet, chopping up an America with a bolo. Incidentally, *bolo* is Philippine Spanish for a heavy work knife, something like the Cuban machete. Christian Filipinos often used it as a weapon. Moros preferred a similar knife called a barong or, more often, a very large kris (an asymmetrical, often wavy dagger) called a sundang or a suluk.

The best-known case of a Filipino absorbing a lot of .38-caliber bullets is that of Antonio Caspi. (Caspi was obviously not a Moro, as Moros had Arabic names.) Caspi was a prisoner on the island of Samar during the Philippine War. Attempting to escape, he was shot four times while fighting with the guards. One .38-caliber bullet hit him in the chest and perforated his right lung. A second bullet punctured his left lung. A third put another hole in his left lung, and a fourth passed through his left hand and arm. Caspi continued to fight until a guard hit him on the head with the butt of a carbine. In three weeks he was discharged from the hospital, cured.

According to Major General Julian S. Hatcher, of the Army Ordnance Corps, an internationally recognized authority on small arms, the Army .38-caliber Colt revolver was a poor weapon. Many of them failed to line up the cylinder and the barrel properly, causing inaccuracy. The cartridge, a .38 long Colt, now obsolete, had a bullet smaller than the diameter of the barrel. The bullet had a hollow base, and the explosion of the powder was supposed to expand it to fit the rifling. This, too, was a source of inaccuracy. The American troops in the Philippines were so unhappy with the (then new) .38-caliber double-action revolvers that the Army dug its old .45-caliber single-action revolvers out of storage and sent them to the Philippines.[6]

The Army wanted a new pistol, and it wanted the new weapon to be .45 caliber. A number of inventors addressed the problem, and John M. Browning, by far the most successful firearms inventor of the period, found the solution. His pistol was adopted in 1911. That was nine years after the day President Theodore Roosevelt announced the end of the war, on July 4, 1902.

So how did the Moros get into this story?

The Moros were exotic. They made a strong impression on the young American troops. The Moros wore traditional Malay clothing and sometimes armor in battle—brass helmets pattered on 16th-century Spanish helmets, and brass mail. They carried swords whether they were in battle or not. They had been fighting Christians on and off for three centuries. Occasionally individual Moros would take an oath to die killing Christians. Before beginning one of these rampages, a Moro usually took large quantities of drugs, which made him hard to kill. American troops stationed in Moroland (the big island of Mindanao and the Sulu Archipeligo) went on guard in threes. One soldier had a .30 rifle, one had a 12-gauge shotgun, and one had an old .45-70 single-shot rifle. The shotgun and .45-70 were chosen for their stopping power. In one case, witnesses reported that a Moro oath-taker managed to kill several people even though he was hit 30 times with projectiles from all three weapons.

The American forces on Mindanao took a number of the datus' forts and quickly quieted the island. The fighting wasn't too hard because most of the Moros had only swords and spears. Then the Sultan of Sulu decided the terms of his treaty with the Americans didn't give him enough, and there was more fighting, but the Moro Crater Massacre in 1906 put an end to it. In the massacre, American troops led by Theodore Roosevelt's buddy, Dr. Leonard Wood, killed 600 Moro men, women, and children hiding in an extinct volcano crater. A few years later, in 1913, Sulu again became restive. This time, troops under Brigadier General John Pershing attacked the Sultan's fort on Bagsak Mountain, and 13 Americans were killed. So were 2,000 Moros, including 196 women and 340 children.

Once again, swords and spears proved no match for machine guns and artillery.

To make this battle seem less like another massacre, Pershing said, "The fighting was the fiercest I have ever seen.... [The Moros] are absolutely fearless and once committed to combat they count death as a mere incident."[7]

That statement, of course, added to the legend of the ferocious Moro.

MYTH #19

The Bayonet Is Indispensible

In the 17th century, the basic infantry force consisted of two types of soldiers: musketeers and pikemen. Then the great French military engineer Sébastien Le Prestre de Vauban caused a revolution in infantry tactics—he improved a weapon that some French musketeers had improvised a few years earlier.

Loading matchlock muskets in those days was a time-consuming activity. The musketeer put some gunpowder from a priming powder container in the pan by the hole in the gun's barrel. He took a wooden powder holder from his bandolier and poured powder into the muzzle of his gun, after which he put a bullet into the muzzle and rammed it down the barrel. Then he blew on his match, a cord which had been soaked in a potassium nitrate solution and dried so it would smolder continuously, to get rid of ashes. The musketeer attached the match to the "serpentine," which held the match on the gun and would lower it into the powder-filled pan, and he prepared to fire. While he was doing all that, he was vulnerable to charging cavalry. His only protection was his fellow soldiers with pikes.

Some unknown musketeer got the idea of ramming a dagger into the muzzle of his musket when he saw the enemy start to charge. That gave him a spear he could use at close quarters. Knifemakers soon began making weapons designed to fit musket muzzles. The city of Bayonne was a knife manufacturing center, and the new weapon became known as a "plug bayonet."[1]

The trouble with the plug bayonet was that the musketeer had to take the dagger out of the gun before he could reload. What Vauban did was either design or promote a new type of bayonet with a sleeve that fit *over* the muzzle of a musket so the

Bayonets of various types and periods. As a weapon in modern war, the bayonet is practically useless, but it's still around.

weapon could be loaded with the bayonet in place. This invention led to the abolition of the pike and therefore doubled the firepower of an infantry unit.

For a century the bayonet was a most important infantry weapon. Few horses could be forced to charge an unbroken fence of bayonets, and still fewer—along with their riders—survived the experience. Cavalry tried attacking infantry from all sides, but the footmen simply formed squares. Against other infantry, the soldiers would fire a volley an instant before they met the enemy, then use their bayonets against the disorganized foe. During the Revolutionary War, "Mad Anthony" Wayne had his men unload their muskets and use their bayonets alone to take the British fort at Stony Point. All through the 19th century and into World War I, troops trained extensively in the use of the bayonet. They thrust at straw-filled dummies and fenced with dummy bayonets with blunt blades mounted on springs.

Nevertheless, use of the bayonet declined steadily as firearms got better. The flintlock musket of the Revolutionary and the Napoleonic Wars was much quicker to load than the old matchlock. General Antoine Jomini, a veteran of Waterloo, said he never saw a bayonet charge in his whole military career, although he had seen troops carry a position without taking their muskets off their shoulders.[2]

When rifles became common, bayonets became even less useful. A rifle could kill at a half-mile or more, which meant that a soldier would be lucky to get within bayonet range of the enemy. An American Civil War surgeon said he had treated only a handful of bayonet wounds.[3]

A French military writer, Colonel Ardent du Pique, in his pre-WWI book, *Etudes sur le Combat*, held that the élan of the French soldier would guarantee success against repeating rifles and machine guns. German writers had a similar theory about the "Furor Teutonicus." When these theories were tested in war, the casualties were enormous, but they were caused by bullets, shrapnel, shell fragments, and poison gas. Of a sample of 200,000 British combat injuries, only 600 were bayonet wounds. A study of wounds suffered by a French corps that had been in extremely heavy close combat in 1916 showed that only .5 percent of the wounds were bayonet wounds. Of all American wounds, only .024 percent were caused by bayonets.[4]

This should have been no surprise to European military theorists. In 1881, in what came to be called the First Boer War, a barely organized rabble of South African farmers, wiped out a British column of 360 regulars positioned on top of Majuba Hill, killing 260 and routing the rest. The South Africans had no bayonets, artillery, or swords.

In the Second Boer War, a few years later, the "Boers" (Dutch for "farmers"), still without bayonets, severely hurt the British regulars, who won the war only by flooding South Africa with more troops than there were men, women, and children in the two South African republics.

All of the Boers were mounted, but their weapons were rifles without bayonets. None of them carried swords or lances, as all European cavalrymen did. Actually, they were not cavalry, but mounted infantry: They rode to the scene of battle and dismounted to fight. When the enemy proved to be too strong, they mounted and rode away.

A British lancer unit did score one victory early in the war, but it was hardly glorious. The lancers charged a group of Boers who were too slow in mounting their horses. The Boers tried to surrender, but the British horsemen ignored their upraised hands and shouts of surrender, and speared the men who had thrown down their rifles, then turned around, rode back, and finished off the wounded prone on the ground.

That never happened again. The Boers were quicker to re-mount, and they also never let an enemy horseman get within lance or sword range.

European officers seemed to think they were modern knights, heirs to an ancient tradition of shock warfare. The infantrymen were warriors as well, heirs to the Greek hoplites and the Roman legionaries. A man was not a warrior unless he was willing to fight hand-to-hand with a sword or a bayonet (which was only a spear that could be used as a rifle).

One of the first Europeans to challenge that tradition was a British veteran of the Second Boer War, Erskine Childers (later a leader in the Irish independence movement). His two books, *The War and the Arme Blanche* and *The German Influence on British Cavalry*, cited instances in the war that, he contended, showed that the cavalry sword should be relegated to museums. He had little more respect for the bayonet. Childers, though, was not a professional soldier.

During the American Civil War, combatants learned the truth at the cost of much blood. Cavalrymen in that war usu-ally fought as mounted infantry, and infantry learned to fear enemy fire at ranges veterans of previous wars would have thought unbelievable. The population of the United States at that time was not much more than a tenth of what it is today, but more Americans died in the Civil War than in all our other wars except World War II.

But even that bloody lesson was forgotten by many American leaders. George S. Patton, Jr., our greatest proponent of armored warfare, designed the last cavalry sword issued to American troops and bitterly protested when the Army stopped issuing swords to horsemen. Swords, though, had become obsolete in Europe as well as America. In the Franco-Prussian War of 1870, the Germans suffered 65,000 casualties, of which swords killed just six men.[5]

Bayonets got shorter, but all armies continued to issue them to all infantrymen. The British fitted their submachine guns with bayonets. The Americans hung them on their semiautomatic M-1 rifle and on both their semiautomatic M-1 carbine and their automatic M-2 carbine. Bayonet drills continued, taking up time that could have been used to improve the generally awful marksmanship of the average soldier.

Bayonet drills were thought to develop an aggressive spirit in infantrymen. Some army and marine units also used the "pugil stick," a stick padded on one end and used by two soldiers wearing crash helmets and face masks to deliver and block blows. That, too, was to foster that aggressive spirit thought so necessary for infantrymen.

No battles have been won by stick fighters since Paleolithic times, of course, and bayonets are not much more useful on automatic rifles with 30-round magazines that can be loaded in a second or two. The U.S. Army has finally dropped the bayonet, but the Marine Corps retains it.

Bless that aggressive spirit.

Myth #20

German Tanks Were Invincible

All of us who are old enough can remember the radio reports on the German invasion of France. (The reporters weren't as excited when the Germans invaded Poland; nobody expected Poland to defeat Germany. But France?!) The Germans broke through the Allied lines and pushed the British and some of the French army into a pocket around Dunkirk, and German tanks ran wild through France. France had generally been considered to have the best army in the world—how could this happen?

Correspondents remembered the previous World War in Belgium and France as a dreary four years in muddy trenches with offensives that gained a few yards one way or the other at the cost of millions of lives. They christened this new method of war the *Blitzkrieg*—German for "lightning war"—and blamed it on the German tanks.

These tanks were monsters (70, 90, 100 tons—their size increased with each report), and they were as numerous as the stars in the sky. Artist conceptions in the Los

Angeles *Examiner* and other newspapers from coast to coast depicted the "frantic efforts" of French and British artillerymen to pierce the armor of these steel juggernauts.

This myth should have had a fairly short life. Even before the war was over, the public learned that there were no 100-ton juggernauts in France. Yet the story hung on. In his memoirs, written well after the war, Winston Churchill said that in 1940 the Germans had at least a thousand "heavy tanks." In fact, they had no heavy tanks at all, and a comparative handful of medium tanks weighing around 20 tons.[1] Most of the Blitzkrieg tanks were light tanks. Toward the end of the war, in 1944, the Germans did come up with a super-juggernaut, nicknamed the Mouse. Actually, there were two juggernauts— only two were built. The "Mice" each weighed 189 tons and fired 155 mm shells. From the tip of its main gun to its back, the Mouse was 33 feet, 9 1/2 inches long. The turret alone weighed 50 tons and was 10 feet wide. Its top speed was 12 1/2 miles per hour. Few bridges could bear its weight, so the Mouse was designed to travel underwater up to 25 feet deep. Both tanks were blown up by the Germans so they wouldn't be captured by the advancing Russians.[2]

German tanks of the Blitzkrieg period bore no resemblance to the Mouse. Historian John Keegan points out in his *The Second World War* that the Blitzkrieg was accomplished by tanks that were in many respects inferior to those of the Allies: "The German tanks were not, model for model, notably superior to those of the British and French armies. The Mark IV Panzer, the army's future main battle tank, was well armored but undergunned. The Mark III, its workhorse, was inferior in protection both to the British Infantry Tank Mark I and the French Somua."[3]

In the invasion of Poland, the vast majority of the German tanks were PanzerKampwagen I and II. The PzKw I weighed less than 6 tons and carried only two 8 mm machine guns. The PzKw II weighed less than 10 tons and carried either a 20 mm or a 37 mm cannon. The PzKw III, the main battle tank used in France, carried either a 37 mm or a 50 mm cannon. The 37 mm gun was entirely inadequate against the heavier Allied tanks. Hitler flew into a rage when he learned that the army was installing 37 mm guns in the Pzkw IIIs instead of 50 mm cannons. As happened many times, the former lance corporal (private first class in American terms) demonstrated more savvy than his generals. (More on this in the next chapter.) The PzKw IV, in short supply during the Blitzkrieg, weighed 21 tons and carried two machine guns and (at that time) one low-velocity 75 mm cannon.[4] The IV underwent many changes during the war, including mounting a long, high-velocity 75 mm gun instead of the short gun on the original model.

The Allies had more tanks on the western front during the Blitzkrieg, and some of them were heavier than anything Germany had. The British "Matilda," for instance, weighed 27 tons, outweighing the PzKw IV by 6 tons. The U.S. M-3 tank, which had been lend-leased to Britain, weighed 27.4 tons and had a hull-mounted 75 mm gun of good length. Another British tank, the "Crusader," weighed 20.1 tons. Further, the Allies had greater numbers of tanks. According to German archives, the German Army had 2,200 tanks in 1940. The French and British had 3,432.[5]

The fact remains, though, that the Germans pushed the British into the sea and conquered France in 19 days. How did that happen?

The two biggest reasons were that the Germans changed:

A U.S. tank in action.
By the time the United States entered World War
II, the Allies had learned how to use tanks.

1. The way tanks were used in combat.

2. The plans for their offensive—at the last minute.

In World War I, the Germans had hardly any tanks, so they were not wedded to traditional tactics. A junior officer, Heinz Guderian, studied the way the Allies had used their tanks in the last war, and theorized in his book *Achtung—Panzer* about how they could have been much more effective. The Allies had distributed their tanks among the infantry, using them as "mobile pillboxes." In so doing, they limited the speed of these machines to the speed of a man on foot. Guderian believed that tanks should be used at the highest speed possible with their internal combustion engines. The Allied formations did not allow tanks to concentrate; Guderian proposed armored divisions with tanks effecting a breakthrough, with motorized infantry able to keep up with the tanks to exploit the breakthrough. Horse-drawn artillery could not be part of a "panzer" (armored) division. Heavy firepower would come from self-propelled artillery and tactical air. For the latter, the Luftwaffe (air force) adopted a technique developed by the U.S. Navy: dive bombing.

In action, the armored divisions used the tactics pioneered by General Oskar von Hutier on the Eastern Front during World War I. Called infiltration tactics, the technique consisted of bypassing strong points, always forging ahead along the lines of least resistance, destroying enemy base areas, and cutting communications and supply lines.

Obviously, the fast-moving panzer divisions could use these tactics far more effectively than divisions of foot-sloggers.

Armored infiltration tactics were made even more effective because the German Army changed its plans. The German Great General Staff had worked out a plan that was a slight variation of the Schlieffen Plan of World War I: A heavily weighted German right wing would invade the Low Countries and swing south and west along the coast and outflank the whole Allied army. It should be noted that the French Maginot Line made it possible for the Germans to concentrate so much strength on the right wing. Manning this long fortified line required a large part of the French Army, and one of the flaws in the line's design was that there was no place along the line from which a major offensive could be launched. The Germans knew that, so they had no fear of a French offensive in that area. They had 19 divisions facing the Maginot line while the French had 59 divisions manning it.[6]

The Allies remembered the Schlieffen Plan too. They remembered that it almost worked, so they greatly increased the strength of their left wing. As soon as the war began, they planned to rush into the Low Countries and smash the Germans before they could get to France.

But not everyone in Germany liked the new Schlieffen Plan. Field Marshal Karl Gerd von Runstedt, one of the most senior generals in the army, didn't like it. Neither did Adolf Hitler, but der Fuhrer was only a lance corporal in the last war and he deferred to the judgment of the professionals of the Great General Staff. Runstedt's chief of staff, Erich von Manstein, agreed with his boss, which might be expected. He not only disagreed with the Great General Staff plan, but he also had an alternative plan that called for an attack just north of the Maginot line, through the Ardennes Mountains. The General Staff said tanks could not attack through the Ardennes. But Manstein consulted Guderian, and the tank expert said it could be done. But it *would* not be done, said the Great General Staff.

Then a plane carrying a staff officer with papers concerning the plan was forced down in Belgium. Thus the plan had to be changed. Monstein's plan was adopted, Guderian led the assault, and France fell.

The 1944 German Blitzkrieg, then, was not due to superior equipment, but superior tactics.

Myth #21

Lance Corporal Hitler Was a Military Moron

During World War II, the U.S. news media delighted in ridiculing Hitler, an ignorant PFC (the same rank as a lance corporal) for trying to tell his generals how to run a war.

Actually, Hitler remembered well that he had never risen above lance corporal in the last war and in fact often deferred to his generals, especially at the beginning of the war. As we saw in the last chapter, when called on to invade the Low Countries and France, the generals opted for a recycled Schlieffen Plan; Hitler favored Manstein's plan, but the generals' plan was dropped—not because Hitler favored another, but because the first plan fell into Allied hands.

Four years later, when the shoe was on the other foot, the generals, including von Runstedt, who had earlier favored Manstein's plan, were certain the Americans and British would try to land at Calais. Hitler thought they'd come to Normandy, but again, he let the generals call the shots—fortunately!

Hitler had some good ideas about weapons too. He urged that the 88 mm antiaircraft gun be remounted and used against tanks as well. It became the most outstanding antitank gun in the war, and mounted in Tiger tank's turret, a superb tank gun as well.

Why Hitler deferred to the generals as much as he did *is* something of a mystery. He should have known from his personal experience in World War I that the military hierarchy can make idiotic mistakes. In that war, Hitler won the Iron Cross but remained at the bottom of the military pecking order. His superiors explained that although Lance Corporal Hitler was a brave soldier, he had no leadership ability!

Adolph Hitler may have been a homicidal maniac, but he often outguessed his generals.

Those poking fun at *der Fuhrer* seemed to forget that a truly evil person is rarely a dunce, and Hitler was about as truly evil as anyone in history. Saints and devils both have talent.

Hitler did have some hang-ups about weapons that sometimes had odd results. For example, he liked *powerful* weapons. That's why he became furious when the army put 37 mm guns in tank turrets that could take 50 mm guns. If you must have weapons, the more powerful ones are usually the right choice.

But then there was the StG 44.

After World War I, German ordnance people decided that their service rifle, the Mauser 98, was too powerful. That didn't seem to be a glaring deficiency during the war, because every other nation's service rifle was also too powerful. The Mauser, like the American Springfield, the British SMLE, the Russian Nagant, and the French Lebel, was accurate at a mile and deadly at even longer range. But how many *soldiers* in a modern mass army were accurate at a mile, or even at half that distance? The price paid for that power was a walloping recoil that made new recruits jerk the trigger or even close their eyes as they fired.

The German ordnance experts knew that fully automatic rifles were just beyond the horizon. The American John Browning had already developed one—the Browning Automatic Rifle (BAR) Model 1918 was a huge, heavy thing, almost 4 feet long and weighing 16 pounds. But the recoil of the powerful .30-06 cartridge made it almost uncontrollable in full automatic fire. The BAR was beefed up so that it finally weighed more than 19 pounds. Still, though, it had to be fired with a bipod and in short bursts to get the best results in full automatic mode. The obvious way to go was not to make the infantryman's rifle heavier than the BAR, but to make his cartridges less powerful.

All armies, especially the German and the Russian, had submachine guns (shoulder-firing weapons with pistol cartridges). They were reasonably controllable in full auto mode, but they were not very effective beyond 100 yards. The new cartridge's power would have to be somewhere between the current service rifle cartridge and a pistol round. Such a cartridge would probably have a shorter case, and the rifle handling it, a shorter action. That could result in both the weapon and its ammunition being lighter. If so, the infantryman could carry more ammunition.

After a lot of experimentation, the Germans came up with a new cartridge and two new rifles, one made by Haenel and one by Walther. They called this new type of infantry weapon a machine carbine (in German, *maschinen karabiner*) and tried them out on the Russian front. The Haenel—called the MKb42—proved to be the better gun and was adopted in 1943 and slated to replace the rifle, the submachine gun, and the light machine gun in the German infantry squad.

When Hitler heard that a rifle using an "intermediate" cartridge would replace the beloved old Mauser, he flew into a rage. The generals calmed the Fuhrer by explaining that the new weapon was just a more powerful submachine gun and would not replace either the rifle or the machine gun. So the new gun became the MP (*maschinen pistole*) 43. Sometime later, Hitler learned that the troops on the eastern front were crazy about the new submachine gun and wanted more of them. So he ordered increased production of the MP 43. He decided that such a powerful weapon should have a more fitting name, and it became Sturmgewehr 44. The English translation of *sturmgewehr* is "assault rifle," Which is now the standard infantry weapon in every country in the world. (*Assault rifle* is also a name that in the United States has been misapplied to ordinary semiautomatic rifles with cosmetic changes that make them look like military weapons.)

Hitler's biggest actual military blunder was his decision to attack Stalingrad. *Stalin* means "steel" in Russian, and Stalingrad at one time was the Pittsburgh of Russia. Hitler, however, took the city to be a symbol of Josef Stalin, his rival for the title of the most evil man in the world. His attack had originally been aimed at the oil fields in the Caucuses, because Germany was running out of fuel. The attack was Germany's only hope of staying in the war, but Hitler blew that chance and lost an army while he was at it. Stalin's ego was as much involved as Hitler's, and Stalin's army was bigger.

The failure at Stalingrad greatly increased the animosity of the army toward Hitler. The army was quite happy with Hitler while it was running roughshod over most of Europe, but when it looked as if they would lose the war, the generals decided to get rid of him. On a visit to the troops in Russia, some officers gave Hitler several bottles of wine. Hitler was not a drinker, so he gave them to an aide, a Colonel Brandt. Brandt apparently was not much of a drinker either, so he gave them to some officers he met on the way back. The wine was poisoned. What happened after that is unknown.

The generals then decided that they could not kill Hitler by remote control; one of them would have to do the deed. But the only one brave enough was Claus von Stauffenberg, a colonel who had lost one arm and had only three fingers on his remaining hand. He couldn't fire a pistol. He would have to use a bomb.

Stauffenberg was carrying the bomb in a briefcase when he joined Hitler and his staff at the Fuhrer's headquarters. Hitler was looking at some plans. Stauffenberg joined the group at the table, standing between Hitler and a heavy post that helped hold up the roof of the headquarters. He put the briefcase there, between Hitler and the post. Then he slipped outside. Inside, Colonel Brandt wanted to get a look at the plans. He tried to squeeze into the place Stauffenberg had occupied, but the briefcase was in the way. He picked it up and put it on the other side of the post.

Outside, Stauffenberg heard the explosion and telephoned his conspirators that the operation was a success. It wasn't. The post had shielded Hitler. Stauffenberg was killed before the day was over, and Hitler responded with a gory massacre of his one-time henchmen.

Nine months later, Hitler took his own life.

Hitler made many mistakes, but if he had followed his generals' advice before the Battle of France or before D-Day, he would have lost the war a lot sooner.

MYTH #22

Nuclear Missiles Are the Ultimate Weapons

The development of the airplane in the early 20th century led to all kinds of prophecies of doom. The most influential of these prophets was probably an Italian artilleryman who never flew in an airplane and had seen only three airplanes in his life before he published an article predicting that the future would see air forces as independent as current armies and navies that would dominate warfare. He proposed that Italy build a fleet of 500 bombers. Such a force, he said, could drop 125 tons of bombs a day and knock out any enemy. Their targets would be factories; roads, railroads, and canals; telephone, telegraph, and radio facilities; government buildings; and population centers. The people in cities hit by explosive and poison gas bombs would, he said, demand that their government make peace.

Others took up the cause. General J.F.C. Fuller, a British military theorist, said it would not be necessary to level cities: "It will be sufficient to have the civilian population driven out so they cannot carry on their usual vocations. A few gas bombs will do that."[1] Another British military commentator, Captain Basil H. Liddell Hart, was much less enthusiastic about gas—mustard gas poisoning during World War I had invalidated him out of the Army. He thought bombing civilian populations was a good idea, however. He recommended bombing the poorer areas of enemy cities. Such bombing, he said, would result in the slum populations being "maddened by the impulse to break loose and maraud."[2]

Air power enthusiasts even predicted that air forces would make traditional armies and navies unnecessary. The British were among the first to establish an independent air force, and the Royal Air Force's (RAF) Bomber Command was dedicated to the strategic bombing of cities. The trouble was that their bombers had short range and couldn't carry many bombs. The Germans, on the other hand, saw their air force as having two roles to play: first, to facilitate the "Blitzkrieg," and second, to defend their cities. They produced medium bombers and dive bombers like the famous *Stuka* and fighter planes like the Bf 109. The British also produced excellent fighter planes like the Hawker Hurricane and the Supermarine Spitfire.

There was some bombing of cities during World War I, with explosives and crude incendiary devices, though no use of gas bombs. In World War II, the first notable bombing of civilians was the Luftwaffe's attacks on Warsaw and on Rotterdam. Rotterdam was a mistake, however; the Dutch authorities were discussing peace with the Germans when the bombs fell.

After the fall of France, the Germans were able to base their short-range planes in Western Europe. They began attacking Britain to soften it up for an invasion. The Germans

U.S. fighter jets releasing bombs.

concentrated on airfields, factories, and naval targets until one night some German planes got lost and released their bombs over blacked-out London. The British responded by raiding Berlin. It wasn't a big raid—the RAF's strength was in fighters, not bombers—but, as the Germans learned, they were still very strong in that department. Hitler, outraged, ordered more attacks on London. That was another of his mistakes. By concentrating on military targets, he might have made possible an invasion of Britain, but by shifting his aim to civilians, he gave up any chance of victory.

Later, when the Germans were busy in Russia, the British switched to bombing German cities, and the Americans joined them when the United States entered the war. The early air raids were not very efficient. The British raids had to be conducted at night, because the British had no long-range fighters to escort their bombers. German cities were all blacked out, and the bomber pilots, relying on intersecting radio beams, sometimes missed whole cities. A British report on bombings of the Ruhr in August 1941 said that only one tenth of the bombers got to within five miles of their assigned targets. The British Air Staff stated that "the only target on which the night force could inflict effective damage was a whole German town."[3]

When the Americans entered the war, they relied on the B-17's firepower and the famous Norden bombsight. The so-called flying fortress's .50-caliber machine guns were an inadequate defense against the cannons and rockets of the German fighters, and the Norden bombsight proved to be the most over-hyped weapon of the war. The Americans soon adopted the British night-bombing strategy, which depended on a greatly improved electronic navigation system. The British also sent specially trained airmen piloting special planes—usually the super-fast, high-altitude Mosquito—to locate targets and drop flares over them. Later, the P-51, an American long-range fighter, brought a resumption of daylight bombing. The P-51, which the British called the Mustang, not only had enough range to escort bombers into eastern Germany, but it was also faster, could fly higher, and was more maneuverable than any German fighter. The Mustang's success induced the British to start daylight bombing again. The British bombers were now much larger and more powerful than those at the beginning of the war, and were capable of dropping the 22,000-pound "Grand Slam" bomb.

The Allied air forces were far more destructive than the Luftwaffe, but the raids didn't do much to affect the German war effort. Vast areas of German cities were obliterated, with 600,000 Germans killed and another 800,000 wounded, but German civilians did not rise up against their government any more than British civilians rose against theirs during the "Blitz."

The bombing's effect on German war production was startlingly ineffective. In 1942, the British dropped 48,000 tons of bombs, and the Germans produced 38,000 heavy weapons (artillery, tanks, and planes). In 1943, the British and Americans dropped 207,600 tons of bombs, and the Germans produced 71,693 heavy weapons. In 1944, the Allies dropped 915,000 tons of bombs, and the German factories turned out 105,258 heavy weapons. German war production continued to increase until 1945, when Allied armies were overrunning the continent of Europe and Germany itself.[4]

Liddell Hart, who had recommended the bombing of enemy slum areas to cause the inhabitants to "break loose and maraud," changed his mind after studying the effects of such bombing. "The potential of the Allied air forces was greater than their achievement," he wrote. "In particular, the British pursued area-bombing long after they had any reason, or excuse, for such indiscriminate action."[5]

While the war was going on in Africa and Europe, the United States was fighting almost single-handed against Japan. The bombing of Tokyo by carrier-based B-25s in 1942 accomplished little material damage, but it was a blow to Japanese morale and led to the disastrous (for Japan) Battle of Midway.

American aircraft carrier fighting off Japanese planes during World War II.

But as the war continued, the United States gained control of Guam, putting the home islands of Japan within range of the B-29 bombers.

General Curtis LeMay inaugurated a new aerial campaign against Japan. The Japanese at this time had almost no fuel, because, as a result of U.S. submarines, surface ships, and planes, they had almost no shipping capabilities. Also, almost all their aircraft factories were gone. As a result, most of their interceptor fighters were also gone. There was no longer any need for high-altitude precision bombing. LeMay's strategy was pure aerial terrorism: low-level night attacks dropping millions of incendiary bombs on the mostly wooden Japanese cities.

On March 8, 1945, 325 B-29s armed exclusively with incendiaries struck Tokyo and Yokohama. They set off the largest firestorm in history. Thousands of people suffocated, because the fire sucked all the oxygen out of the air. At least 267,000 buildings burned to the ground—about 16 square miles of densely populated urban area—and the heat of the firestorm made water in the cities' canals boil. The death toll from that one raid came to 89,000, or 20,000 more than all the British dead from air attacks in the entire war. The fire raids went on and on. By July, 60 percent of the area of the country's 60 largest cities had been burned out. But the Japanese people were not clamoring for their government to make peace.

By this time, the United States had nuclear bombs, and the Americans targeted Hiroshima and Nagasaki, two small cities with no military or industrial objectives—all the worthwhile targets in Japan had already been obliterated. On August 6, 1945, the first atomic bomb exploded over Hiroshima, killing 78,000 people. Three weeks later, the second bomb struck Nagasaki, killing 25,000.

Yet *neither* raid was as deadly as the one on Tokyo, and they could not compare with the fatalities and damage caused by the series of fire-bomb raids. But they did give the Japanese government a face-saving excuse to ask for peace.

**The last bomb of World War II: An atom
bomb explodes over Nagasaki.**

Japan is an island nation. It was isolated, without ships,
fuel, or airplanes. Its people were hungry; millions of them,
homeless. But they would not surrender until their emperor
gave the word. Several atomic bombs could not have made

them worse off than they already were. The pre-war predictions of Giulio Douhet and his followers proved to be so much hot air. Would a future use of nuclear weapons change that? Unlikely, but pray that we never find out.

Myth #23

Douglas MacArthur Was Our Greatest Military Hero

On April 10, 1951, General of the Army Douglas MacArthur was relieved of his command of the U.S. Far East Command. The event, if not earth-shaking, certainly shook the nation, especially the political elite in Washington. Congressional Republicans began talking about the general as a potential candidate for president. MacArthur's nemesis, President Harry Truman, was, at the time, the least popular president in two decades.

Then the MacArthur boom began to fizzle. The Senate Armed Services Committee looked into the dismissal and concluded that President Truman had acted correctly. Publisher Henry Luce, a longtime MacArthur fan, wanted to make MacArthur *Time's* Man of the Year. His editors talked him out of it.

What happened?

In the course of his 52-year military career, MacArthur had probably received more favorable publicity than any other public figure. Luce's publications, *Time*, *Life*, and

Fortune, practically canonized him. Even foreign writers sang his praises (although at times, somewhat off-key). For example, A.J.P. Taylor, a greatly respected British historian says, "It was a high irony of war that General MacArthur should follow a flexible maritime strategy while Admiral Nimitz continued to think in conventional military terms."[1] (This, although Nimitz island-hopped his way across the Pacific, bypassing such Japanese strongholds as Truk.) B.H. Liddell Hart, another Briton, says, of MacArthur, "His combination of strong personality, strategic grasp, tactical skill, operative mobility and vision put him in a class above Allied commanders in any theater." That's an assessment that his record will show is more than a little exaggerated.[2] Two other British historians, John Keegan and Andrew Wheatcroft, call him not only handsomer than his father, another noted general, but "one of the most physically striking of all Great Captains," which verges on the ridiculously fulsome.[3]

If Douglas MacArthur did not live up to the estimates of his adoring fans, he was still far from insignificant. He was a brilliant man who graduated at the top of his West Point class. He was a brave man who received a staggering number of medals. He was an astute politician, a master of the office politics of the Department of the Army and later of the Department of Defense, and extraordinarily effective as the de facto Shogun of Occupied Japan.

MacArthur came from a talented family. His grandfather was a Scottish immigrant who became a judge. His father, Arthur MacArthur, Jr., won the Medal of Honor for his heroism on Missionary Ridge in the Civil War while a teenager, and eventually became the U.S. Army's highest-ranking general. Douglas's brother, Arthur MacArthur III, won the Navy Cross and the Distinguished Service Medal as well as command of a battleship before he died in 1923.

Arthur MacArthur, Jr. was commanding general in the Philippines during the Philippine War and reluctantly endorsed the cloak-and-dagger expedition of Brigadier General Frederick Funston that captured Philippine President Emilio Aguinaldo. Funston and four other officers were to go to Aguinaldo's head-quarters disguised as prisoners of war, escorted by a company of Filipinos who were loyal to the Americans.

"Funston, this is a desperate undertaking. I fear I shall never see you again," MacArthur said.[4]

But Funston succeeded. Aguinaldo surrendered and so did most of his officers. In spite of howls from the States to hang Aguinaldo, MacArthur befriended the ex-president and one of his aides, a very young man named Major Manuel Quezon who later became president of the Philippines.

In spite of his achievements, Arthur MacArthur was not without his critics. Colonel Enoch H. Crowder, one of his aides, said, "Arthur MacArthur was the most flamboyantly egotistical man I had ever seen, until I met his son."[5]

Arthur MacArthur's death could not have been more theatrical. His old Civil War Regiment, the 24th Wisconsin, held its annual reunion on Sept. 5, 1912. Only 90 veterans of Missionary Ridge were still alive. Arthur MacArthur, the regiment's former commander, was to give the main address. He was just beginning his summary when he collapsed on the stage. Dr. William J. Cronyn, who had been the regiment's surgeon, leaped up on the stage and examined the old soldier.

"Comrades," he said, "The general is dying."[6] The Rev. Paul B. Jenkins, who had been the regiment's chaplain, led the veterans in the Lord's Prayer. When they were finished,

Dr. Cronyn told them the general was dead. Retired Captain Edward Parsons went to the wall and took down the tattered flag MacArthur had carried up Missionary Ridge. He covered the general's body with it, and then he, too, keeled over. Two weeks later, he was dead.

The son, Douglas MacArthur, had seen action in the Philippines in 1903. He was caught in an ambush and, he said, he killed two Filipino guerrillas. Two years after his father's death he would be involved in some spectacular intelligence action.

The Mexican Revolution, which began in 1910, had re-sulted in an unscrupulous general named Victoriano Huerta seizing the presidency. Woodrow Wilson, who thought all Mexicans were inferior beings who needed advice from the United States, hated him and refused to recognize his govern-ment. On April 10, 1914, some American sailors, who landed at Tampico to pick up gasoline they had previously ordered, were erroneously arrested. Before the Mexican troops could take them anywhere, an officer appeared and released them. The officer apologized profusely. So did the commander of the Tampico garrison.

That wasn't enough for Admiral Henry T. Mayo. Without consulting anyone in Washington, he sent an ultimatum to Huerta himself, demanding that he "publicly hoist the American flag in a prominent place and salute it with twenty-one guns."[7]

The demand was unprecedented in international law, but PresidentWilson backed up Mayo. Huerta refused to salute the flag of a foreign government that would not admit the exis-tence of his own.

Then Washington heard that a German ship was en route to Veracruz with weapons for Huerta's army. Wilson ordered the U.S. Navy to occupy Veracruz, so it did.[8] Later, Wilson sent Army troops to Veracruz for a long-term occupation. Commanding them was Brigadier General Frederick Funston, who had captured Aguinaldo in the Philippines.

At this point, war with Mexico became a distinct possibility. Major General Leonard Wood, the Army chief of staff, decided he needed more information about the Veracruz area. He sent his aide, Captain Douglas MacArthur, to Veracruz to get it. MacArthur was to talk to no one, not even Funston. So Wood was ignoring Frederick Funston, the most successful cloak-and-dagger operator in the Army's history—Leonard Wood, whose most notable achievement in the Philippines was the slaughter of 900 men, women, and children in the infamous Moro Crater Massacre.

MacArthur went to Veracruz. In case of war, the port city would be an obvious point of entry for an invasion force. It was also a rail center, and there were plenty of railroad cars in the rail yards, but no locomotives. MacArthur hired three Mexicans for $150 in gold and borrowed a railroad handcart to look for the missing engines. MacArthur wore his U.S. Army uniform so he could not be accused of being a spy.

First, he searched the men for weapons and got a knife and a revolver. Then he allowed them to search him. They found that he had no money and his only weapon was a tiny Remington double derringer, an easily concealable weapon that was a favorite of Western gamblers. He kept the derringer.

The derringer was effective at the range of a few feet, but it was extremely inaccurate, had little power, and less penetration. Its .41 rimfire cartridge had about 78 foot-pounds of muzzle energy—less than an ordinary .22 long rifle cartridge. The late Elmer Keith, a famous firearms authority, says somewhere in his book *Sixguns* that unless it hit squarely, a bullet from the little Remington would not penetrate a tin can.[9]

MacArthur and the Mexicans found five locomotives in Alvarado. On the way back, he reported, they were attacked by five armed men. They were able to outrun all but two, whom MacArthur said he shot with his little derringer. A little later, 15 men attacked them, and, MacArthur said, he shot four of them, and they retired. Three more men then attacked them, but they outran all but one. MacArthur said he shot both that man and his horse. The horse fell across the tracks and had to be dragged off them. When MacArthur reported in, he had several bullet holes in his clothes.

For this feat, MacArthur was nominated for the Medal of Honor, the nation's highest award. But probably because of the improbable details of his story—killing a horse and shooting seven horsemen with his tiny derringer—he was not given the medal. The board considering it, however, said that "to bestow the award recommended might encourage any other staff officer, under similar conditions, to ignore the local commander, possibly interfering with the latter's plans."[10] That would be a reasonable cause for rejection if the expedition were MacArthur's idea. But it wasn't. The board's rejection, though, was better than calling the son of the Army's highest-ranking general a liar. Either way, MacArthur got no award at all.

In World War I, MacArthur was promoted to major, then colonel, and made chief of staff for the 42nd Division. He was no pompous, cartoonish Colonel Blimp. He took part in trench raids and helped capture enemy prisoners. He was promoted to brigadier general. He won the Distinguished Service Cross, five Silver Stars, two *Croix de Guerre* and a *commandant* of the *Legion d'honneur*. He was wounded and again nominated for the Medal of Honor. Instead, he got another Distinguished Service Cross. MacArthur was known as "the Beau Brummel of the AEF." He altered his cap to give it the "40 mission crush" look later popular with pilots in World War II and wore a brightly colored pull-over sweater. At one point he was captured by American soldiers who thought he was a German general. A day before the armistice he was made commander of the 42nd Division.

In peacetime, MacArthur was commandant of West Point, and he served again in the Philippines where he renewed old friendships, including with his father's friend, Manuel Quezon. He became the Army's youngest major general. In 1930, he became Army Chief of Staff. In 1935, the Philippines became semi-independent, Quezon, the Philippine president, asked MacArthur to become field marshal of the Philippine Army. He accepted, and for a time he drew the pay of both a U.S. major general and a Philippine field marshal until his retirement from the U.S. Army in 1937.

In the late 1930s, war clouds were gathering over both the Atlantic and the Pacific. There was a general feeling among troops in the Pacific and among almost everyone in the U.S. Navy that the United States would soon be at war with Japan, especially after the Japanese bombed and sank the navy gunboat *Panay* on the Yangtze River. MacArthur and Quezon asked the United States for aid for the Philippine armed forces. They got some, but not enough. Instead of combat boots, for example, the Filipino soldiers got sneakers.[11]

Although many people worried about a Japanese attack on the Philippines, MacArthur was the soul of optimism. He said he did not believe the Japanese would attack, and if they did, he was confident the Philippines could defend itself. As world conditions grew more ominous, President Franklin Roosevelt called MacArthur back from retirement and federalized the Philippine Army. When World War II broke out in Europe, the United States committed itself to a "Europe first" policy, and plans for the defense of the Philippines were scaled back. "Plan Orange" was adopted, which called for a concentration around Manila, chiefly the Bataan Peninsula and the island fortress of Corregidor. MacArthur ignored Plan Orange and distributed his forces around the archipelago.

While Japanese carrier planes were attacking Pearl Harbor, other Japanese aircraft were massing on Formosa (Taiwan today). It was nighttime in the Philippines and Formosa during the Pearl Harbor raid. The Japanese planned to take off from Formosa at 2:30 a.m. so they would be over the Philippines at daybreak, but they couldn't take off because of a tremendous fog. Japanese commanders were afraid that American planes from the Philippines would catch them on the ground.

MacArthur had received orders on November 19 that if hostilities broke out he should attack any Japanese forces in range. When he learned of the attack on Pearl Harbor, Major General Lewis Brereton, commander of MacArthur's air forces, tried to get MacArthur's approval to bomb the Japanese planes on Formosa. MacArthur's chief of staff, Brigadier General. Richard Sutherland, would neither let him see MacArthur nor give his approval to Brereton's plan. Brereton tried again after he learned that Japanese carrier planes had bombed a U.S. Naval ship off the southern island of Mindanao. Same result.

MacArthur finally approved a bombing attack at 11 a.m. Brereton ordered his planes to land for refueling. They were still refueling when the Japanese arrived at 12:20 p.m. and destroyed most of them on the ground. The U.S. Navy ships in the Philippines, deprived of air cover, took off.

At Pearl Harbor, Admiral Husband Kimmel and General Walter Short were taken by surprise. The rage they inspired by being unprepared was tremendous. There was talk of courts-martial. That didn't happen, but both were retired immediately. In the Philippines, MacArthur had *nine hours warning*. Then the Japanese invaded and cornered his more numerous forces in the Bataan Peninsula. MacArthur wasn't court-martialed. He wasn't retired. He was made supreme commander of the Allied forces in the Southwest Pacific.

The Japanese Philippine invasion force numbered 129,435; MacArthur's troop strength was about 151,000. But the American and Filipino troops were not as well equipped and less well trained. The responsibility for their poorer equipment belongs to the penury of the U.S. government and its "Europe first" policy, but much of the responsibility for the lack of training belongs to Douglas MacArthur.

The American and Filipino troops retreated to the Bataan Peninsula where they were to hold out for three months. MacArthur, his family, Quezon, and MacArthur's staff holed up in Corregidor, where MacArthur acquired his nickname, "Dugout Doug."

On March 11, 1942, MacArthur, his family, and his staff were evacuated from the Philippines and taken to Australia for his new post as commander in the Southwest Pacific. He was also awarded the Medal of Honor for which he had been twice unsuccessfully nominated. The stated reason? To raise the morale of the troops.

MacArthur's last message to Jonathan "Skinny" Wainwright, who took over command, was: "I am utterly opposed under any circumstances or conditions to the ultimate capitulation of this command. If food fails, you will prepare and execute an attack upon the enemy."[12]

For the rest of the war MacArthur performed competently, although, as usual, he was quick to claim credit even when none was due. For instance, he claimed a victory in the Battle of the Coral Sea, although the only participation by his forces was an attack by land-based bombers who scored no worthwhile hits. All of the effective fighting was done by Navy ships and planes not under his command.

He became military governor of Occupied Japan, where he demonstrated his brilliance as a politician. About the only black mark on his reign was his treatment of Yamashita Tomoyuki. Yamashita, "the Tiger of Malaya," was the leading Japanese war hero. MacArthur apparently wanted to hang a war criminal before the Allies in Nuremburg did, so Yamashita was convicted of atrocities committed by Japanese naval forces in Manila while he was completely cut off from them.

Then came the Korean War and MacArthur's downfall.

At the Yalta Agreement, the Allies treated Korea as if it were a colonial possession of Japan instead of a liberated nation. It was to be governed by a trusteeship composed of the U.S., Britain, China, and the U.S.S.R. In reallity, it was actually divided into United States (South Korea) and Soviet (North Korea) zones. MacArthur, busy trying to turn Japan into a democracy, cared little about Korea. He seemed to think it was conquered territory and refused to let it have an army with heavy weapons. The Russians, on the other hand, set up a Communist state with Russian-born Kim Il Sung as dictator.[13]

North Korea got Russian tanks, artillery, and infantry weapons, and its soldiers were trained by Russian veterans of the recent war. When Kim sent them across the southern border, the South Koreans could do little to stop them. At the time, the Soviet Union was boycotting the United Nations, so it couldn't veto the UN Security Council's decision to intervene militarily and make MacArthur commander of UN forces.

MacArthur's American forces owned the air and the sea, but they couldn't stop the North Koreans from moving down that mountainous, forested peninsula. MacArthur had four Army divisions in Japan, but they were scattered and equipped more for occupation duties than for war. They were rushed to Korea as more troops began arriving there from the United States. It would be some time before troops from other UN nations would arrive (and not many ever did). American and South Korean troops formed a perimeter around the big southern port of Pusan, and, eventually, some UN troops arrived to strengthen the line.

MacArthur proposed an amphibious landing farther up the peninsula to get behind the North Koreans massed around Pusan. "The remarkable thing about this plan is that it is what the situation practically demanded, and yet MacArthur had to fight a dogged battle with the top American military leadership, the Joint Chiefs of Staff, to get it approved," wrote combat historian Bevin Alexander.[14]

The Japanese had used this tactic repeatedly when moving down the Malay Peninsula. The United States had even more experience in amphibious tactics in the Pacific war. But the Joint Chiefs remembered the Anzio beachhead, a fiasco that just missed being a disaster, during the war in Europe. MacArthur pointed out that at Inch'on where he would land troops there were almost no North Korean forces; almost all the North Korean troops were in the south, around Pusan. The only problems at Inch'on were the tides and the mud flats: The difference between high and low tide was 35 feet, and when the tide was out, it exposed mile-wide mud flats that would stop

MacArthur observes the landing off of Inch'on, Korea.

any boat or any land vehicle and probably could not even be walked on.

But MacArthur had a secret weapon to take care of the tides and the mud. Its name was Eugene F. Clark, a Navy lieutenant (the equivalent of an Army captain). Clark was a "mustang," a Navy officer who had once been an enlisted man. He was an expert on the Korean coast and experienced in intelligence operations. Clark and two South Korean officers sneaked into Inch'on Harbor and gathered information on tides and potential landing spots while organizing local people into a guerrilla force and even fighting a naval battle with machine gun–armed junks.

The landing turned out to be a piece of cake. One result of that, according to Lieutenant Geneneral Matthew B. Ridgway, "was the development of an almost superstitious regard for General MacArthur's infallibility. Even his superiors, it seemed, began to doubt if they should question *any* of MacArthur's decisions."[15]

With the Americans in their rear, the North Koreans retreated precipitously. The Americans followed. MacArthur designated the Inch'on landing force "X Corps" and gave its command to Major General Edward "Ned" Almond, his chief of staff. Almond was a typical MacArthur staff officer, sycophantic toward the Great Man and arrogant toward everyone else. After the Inch'on landing, ships took X Corps around to the east coast while the Eighth Army (the rest of the U.S. troops) proceeded up the west coast. The two units had only tenuous contact.

At this point, the North Koreans were all out of South Korea. MacArthur had no UN mandate to invade North Korea, but he decided to unify Korea. Truman seemed to agree with him. The Chinese warned that if the UN forces reached the Yalu River, the border between Korea and China, they would have to intervene.

MacArthur scoffed at the notion of Chinese intervention. He boasted that he understood "the Oriental mind." He knew the Chinese would not intervene—just as he knew that the Japanese would never invade the Philippines. When his troops on the Yalu captured some Chinese prisoners, he didn't change his mind. They were just a few volunteers, he said.

The Chinese government said the Chinese in Korea were volunteers too. Four field armies with their entire command structure intact, plus all their artillery, machine guns, and mortars, were all volunteers, and the Chinese government was not involved. Later, American troops on R&R (rest and recuperation for a week) could go to Hong Kong across the border into

China and visit the homeland of the troops they were fighting in Korea.

Those four Chinese armies slipped through gaps in the UN line, especially the big gap between X Corps and the Eighth Army. They drove the UN forces down the peninsula almost as fast as the UN forces had driven the North Koreans up it.

"Dugout Doug" hit the panic button. Six days after the Chinese offensive began, MacArthur cabled the Joint Chiefs that unless he got heavy reinforcements, his army would be confined to a tiny beachhead, and then, "facing the entire Chinese nation," would be destroyed.[16]

The Chiefs said, "We believe that we should not commit our remaining available ground forces to action against the Chinese Communist forces in Korea in the face of the increased threat of a general war." They recommended that he fight from a succession of defensive positions.[17]

MacArthur next proposed that the United States recognize that it was at war with China, not just some Chinese "volunteers"—who were eventually to consist of eight or nine field armies. It could then blockade China, bomb its cities and factories, and have Chinese Nationalists from Taiwan join the fight in Korea and raid the coast of mainland China. He did not see that a blockade of China, given its enormous land border with the Soviet Union, would be useless, would enrage allies like the British, who would lose contact with Hong Kong, and would never be approved by the United Nations. China at that time was not the industrial power it is today; some Chinese soldiers had only a half-dozen hand grenades, and they were expected to pick up the guns of fallen comrades—they had few factories to bomb. As for Chinese Nationalists, South Korean President Syngman Rhee said if they came to Korea, he would pull his South Korean troops out of the front lines and drive

Chiang Kai-shek's (Nationalist China's political and military leader) men into the sea.

MacArthur sent a cable about the condition of his army. "The troops are tired from a long and difficult campaign, embittered by the shameful propaganda which has falsely condemned their courage and fighting qualities in misunderstood retrograde maneuver, and their morale will become a serious threat to their battle efficiency unless the political basis upon which they are asked trade life for time is clearly delineated, fully understood, and so impelling that the hazards of battle are cheerfully accepted."[18]

If anyone was casting unjust aspersions on his men, it was MacArthur himself. He knew nothing about the morale of the troops, because he rarely came to Korea.

It was true that their morale was not the highest during the constant retreating of December 1950, but now the troops on the ground had a new commander, Matthew B. Ridgway. The troops had a new outlook, and they were fighting a new war.

When he got to Korea, Ridgway was shocked by what he saw. Food was in short supply and frequently delayed. Soldiers had no winter uniforms. Units had been flanked because there were no friendly troops beside them. To the ordinary GIs, that meant that the brass wasn't doing its job. Ridgway moved the field kitchens closer to the line. He ordered more winter clothing. He told his unit commanders to stay in touch with those on their flanks, even if it meant using smoke signals. He told Ned Almond that X Corps was still part of the Eighth Army and that he, Ridgway, was part of the chain of command and gave the orders to X Corps, not the FECOM commander. He told the officers to get their troops off the road and into the hills. He brought up a lot more armor and artillery to take advantage of the Eighth Army's vastly superior firepower.

And he counterattacked. While MacArthur was moaning about being forced into a tiny beachhead and being destroyed, the Eighth Army was advancing. It recaptured Seoul and was a short hop from the 38th Parallel.

Things looked much brighter for the UN campaign. Things looked so bright that Truman thought that the North Koreans and Chinese might be receptive to a cease fire. The Joint Chiefs sent MacArthur this message:

> State planning presidential announcement shortly that, with clearing bulk of South Korea of aggressors, United Nations now prepared to discuss conditions of settlement in Korea. Strong UN feeling persists that further diplomatic effort towards settlement [should continue] before any advance with major forces north of the 38th parallel. Time will be required to determine diplomatic reactions and permit new negotiations that may develop. Recognizing that parallel has no military significance, State has asked JCS what authority you should have to permit sufficient freedom of action for the next few weeks to provide security for UN forces and maintain contact with enemy. Your recommendations desired.[19]

MacArthur replied that his present directives were sufficient, but he probably ground his teeth. If the war ended now, he would not win a great victory. He really wanted a war with China, but that was exactly what Washington was trying to avoid. With the increasingly unstable Josef Stalin, a war with China could lead to World War III. Both the United States and the Soviet Union had hundreds of nuclear weapons—the potential death and destruction was mind-boggling.

So before Truman could give his address, MacArthur issued an announcement of his own:

"Even under the inhibitions which now restrict the activity of the United Nations forces and the corresponding military advantages which accrue to Red China, it has shown its complete inability to accomplish by force of arms the conquest of Korea," he said. That was not mere bombast. It was intended to insult the Chinese. MacArthur switched to his own "peace proposal": "The enemy now must be painfully aware that a decision of the United Nations to depart from its tolerant effort to contain the war to the area of Korea through the expansion of our military operations to his coastal areas and interior bases would doom Red China to the risk of imminent military collapse." Finally, he set himself up as the ultimate authority: "Within my area of authority as military commander, however, it should be needless to say I stand ready at any time to confer in the field with the commander-in-chief of the enemy forces in an earnest effort to find any military means whereby the realization of the political objectives of the United Nations in Korea, to which no nation may justly take exception, might be accomplished without further bloodshed."[20]

You didn't have to be an expert on "the Oriental mind" to know that MacArthur's arrogant and insulting tone would prevent the Communist authorities from ever considering Truman's peace initiative. Truman was enraged not because of MacArthur's arrogance, but because he had deliberately sabotaged national policy. MacArthur's pronouncement meant that the war would continue for another two years and kill some 20,000 more American soldiers as well as literally millions of Koreans (both north and south) and Chinese.

MacArthur, a hero?

Myth #24

Harry Truman Desegregated the Armed Forces in 1948

On July 26, 1948, President Harry Truman issued an executive order: "It is hereby declared to be the policy of the president that there shall be equality of treatment and opportunity for all persons in the armed services without regard to race, color, religion or national origin. This policy shall be put into effect as rapidly as possible and having due regard to the time required to effectuate any necessary changes without impairing efficiency or morale."

The order was an enormous step forward for the U.S. armed forces and for the president himself—Truman came from a state that had more than a tinge of the Deep South. During the Civil War, Truman's mother and grandmother had been interned in a camp for Confederate sympathizers. While he was in high school in Independence, Missouri, a Kansas City suburb, one of the local newspapers, the *Jackson County Examiner*, editorialized: "The community at large need not be especially surprised if there is a negro lynching in Independence.... There are a lot of worthless young negro men who do nothing. They do not pretend to work and stand around on the streets and swear and make remarks about ladies and other who may pass by. They crowd into the electric cars and become offensive."[1]

Growing up surrounded by this kind of prejudice had an effect on the president. In 1918, he said that New York was a "kike town" that was also filled with "wops." He admitted that he had racial prejudice: "I am strongly of the opinion that negroes ought to be in Africa, yellow men in Asia, and white men in Europe and America."[2]

At one point, Truman's sister, Mary Jane, said, "Harry is no more for nigger equality than any of us."[3] And in casual conversation for many years terms like *nigger, coon, bohunk, chink,* and *jap* sprinkled his conversation. But language was one thing; action was another. Truman was outraged by obvious injustice. He was greatly disturbed by the internment of Japanese Americans during World War II. He compared it to the internment of his Confederate sympathizing ancestors.

When in 1946 black soldiers were being dragged out of Army trucks and beaten, Truman said, "My very stomach turned over."[4] He was absolutely horrified when Sergeant Isaac Woodward was arrested at a bus stop in Georgia because the bus driver said he took too long in the "colored only" restroom. The police charged him with drunkenness, although he had had nothing to drink, and beat him with a blackjack and a club so severely that he became blind.

"I had no idea it was as terrible as that," Truman told Walter White of the NAACP. "We've got to do something." Something was hard to do. Southerners in the Senate and

House of Representatives fought desperately against any attempt to improve life for the African American population. Truman could make no progress with Congress, so he tried an executive order. As commander-in-chief of the armed forces, he could act without approval of Congress.

But the part of his order regarding the time required to effectuate change was a catch-22. Many senior officers seemed to think that that time would be at least a century. Douglas MacArthur, the most senior officer, certainly did; segregation during the Korean War did not end until Matthew Ridgway took over the Far East Command (FECOM). Under Ridgway, the 24th Infantry Regiment, the last of the "Buffalo Soldiers"—two infantry regiments and two cavalry regiments that were formed after the Civil War and served mostly on the western frontier (they got their nickname from the Native Americans who thought the curling hair on the black soldiers' scalps resembled that on the buffalo's scalp)—was desegregated.

Although the desegregation order was signed in 1948, desegregation did not become a fact for another four years. The demise of the "Buffalo Soldiers" ended a long and dishonorable tradition.

In the Civil War, 186,000 African Americans served in the Army, and another 30,000 in the Navy. All of the Army units were segregated with black enlisted men and mostly white officers. African Americans in the Navy were almost all enlisted men. After the war, many people wanted to make the armed services all lily-white, even though black men had fought in all U.S. wars since the fighting at Concord and on Bunker Hill. It was considered a major concession to allow the four segregated regiments.

The Buffalo Soldiers rescued Teddy Roosevelt's "Rough Riders" at Las Guaysimas and beat them to the top of Kettle Hill in the Spanish American War, but in his account of the war, Roosevelt slandered them. In World War I, the Army formed two black combat divisions, but General John Pershing palmed off the troops in one division to the French army—after cautioning the French not to become too familiar with the African Americans (advice the French ignored). The other division Pershing did his best to keep out of combat. In spite of the black soldiers' contributions in the Civil War and the Spanish War, the Army brass professed to believe that black soldiers couldn't fight.

In World War II, all black soldiers were in segregated units, and most of them were truck drivers, engineers (military speak for laborers), and other non-combat jobs.

Harry Truman certainly did desegregate the armed forces, but it wasn't, as the myth has it, instantly done with the stroke of a pen.

MYTH #25

There Was No Korean War After Peace Talks Began

The Korean War has been called—accurately—"the Forgotten War." One of the reasons it has been forgotten is that the U.S. government, for some unknown reason, seems to have tried to erase the memory of most of it.

After the peace talks began, the Pentagon rarely mentioned any fighting by North Korean troops. Several years ago I was writing a magazine article about a rather small, bloody action at a place officially called Listening Post Alice or Agnes and more commonly known as Sandbag Castle. The fighting around Sandbag Castle was typical of the little-publicized actions after the peace talks began that contributed to the post-peace-talk total of 82,500 American casualties out of 157,530 in the whole war.[1]

Sandbag Castle was a strange product of the cease-fire talks at Panmunjom. Unlike MacArthur, Ridgway was not primarily concerned with taking territory—he wanted to kill enemies. If he had to advance to get within maximum killing range of the enemy forces, he would advance. The Chinese and North Koreans built deep and elaborate fortifications, especially in the eastern mountains. That's where the brunt of the UN forces' "meat grinder" offensive fell. Those mountains acquired appropriate nicknames like "Bloody Ridge" and "Heartbreak Ridge." The UN forces had moved about 20 miles into North Korea at the cost of thousands of casualties. But the Communist forces had suffered even heavier casualties because of the enormous UN firepower.

It was apparent that offensive operations against lines of trenches and bunkers was expensive, even when one side had overwhelming numbers of cannons and exclusive possession of tanks and modern aircraft. So the Joint Chiefs ordered Ridgway and the Eighth Army commander, James Van Fleet, to hold the line, not advance.

At the time, the Turkish Brigade was holding part of Heartbreak Ridge. The Turks were told not to advance beyond their trenches. So what they did was advance their trenches. They dug a trench toward the North Korean main line of resistance, roofed it with steel fence posts and sandbags, and protected it with flanking bunkers that were connected to the main tunnel with flanking tunnels. When they were ordered to stop, they built an enormous, towering bunker at the end of the tunnel. That was Sandbag Castle, located only 10 yards from the North Korean trenches. When the Turks moved elsewhere, the 27th Infantry Regiment inherited Sandbag Castle.

The UN held the line everywhere, and the Communist forces vainly tried to break through with a series of offensives in 1952 and 1953. There were no more big pushes in the eastern mountains, but there were a large number of company- and battalion-sized attacks everywhere. Sandbag Castle was the scene of a number of small attacks. On September 5, 1952, the North Koreans launched a bigger-than-usual attack. They opened by dropping 1,200 mortar shells, including the huge 120 mm shells, on Sandbag Castle and then attacked that tiny bunker complex with a whole battalion.

The fighting involved one company of the 27th Infantry Regiment and a battalion of the KPA (Korean Peoples Army) or the North Korean Army. Because of it, one American machine gunner got the Medal of Honor (posthumously) and every North Korean in the attacking force died.

I had been at Sandbag Castle the morning after, taking pictures. So had a major from battalion headquarters who came up to look over the scene. The first sergeant of the company involved was showing him around.

"Keep your head down, sir" the sergeant said. "The snipers are still active."

Instead of keeping low, the major climbed up on a trench parapet and looked around. He turned around and faced the sergeant.

"I don't see anyth—"

Those were his last words.

Researching the article years after Sandbag Castle, I looked up an old copy of the *New York Times* in the local library to see what had been reported. I found that the Pentagon told the press that the *Chinese* had attacked Sandbag Castle. There were no Chinese in that part of Korea.

The Army tried hard to give the impression that after the Inch'on landing and the push to the Yalu. the North Korean Army had ceased to exist. And after the peace talks began, it downplayed any news of fighting. It was almost impossible to get a story about any sort of combat in *Pacific Stars and Stripes* (a newspaper that should not be confused with the *Stars and Stripes* of World War II). *Pacific Stars and Stripes* never questioned any Pentagon policy. The only exception to the "no combat" freeze was when two National Guard divisions, the 40th and 45th, joined us. Publicity for the National Guard was politically correct.

Since the "yoyo days" ("I been up and down this peninsula like a yoyo," the old-timers used to say) were over, the news media seemed uninterested in the war. Consequently, a lot of people were not aware of it. But the ignorance of the U.S. population was nothing compared to that of American troops stationed in Europe.

Back home, preparing to be mustered out, we Korean vets were reunited with guys we hadn't seen in two years. They were full of war stories about how they had been "on the line" in Germany, looking at real, live Communists. They had no idea that we had been *shooting at* real, live Communists who were also shooting at us. Most of their news, of course, came from media controlled by the military.

Myth #26

Dwight Eisenhower Ended the Korean War

This myth has been around for years. The gist of it is that President Dwight Eisenhower stopped the seemingly endless war and equally endless peace negotiations at Panmunjom by threatening to use the atomic bomb in North Korea. Ronald B. Frankum and Stephen F. Maxner mention it in their *The Vietnam War for Dummies* with a section called "Ike to the Rescue."

The truth is not so simple. If a threat to use nuclear weapons could have ended the war, the fighting would have stopped after Harry Truman told the press that the United States "will take whatever steps are necessary to meet the military situation...."

A reporter asked, "Will that include the atomic bomb?"

"That includes every weapon we have," the President said.

"Mr. President, you said, 'Every weapon we have.' Does that mean that there is active consideration of the use of the atomic bomb?"

"There has always been active consideration of its use. I don't want to see it used. It is a terrible weapon and should not be used on innocent men, women, and children who have nothing whatever to do with this military aggression—that happens when it's used."[1]

That press conference took place November 30, 1950, more than two years before Eisenhower moved into the White House. At the time, there were still worthwhile targets in North Korea. Near the end of the war, but before Eisenhower took office, North Korea had been bombed as flat at Japan in World War II. Because there were no significant buildings left to bomb, U.S. planes began bombing dams to flood the North Korean farmlands.

Truman realized that he was scaring most of the world half to death—atomic bombs meant World War III, people believed—so he took his statement back. In a way.

"[Use of the atomic bomb] is a matter that the military people will have to decide. I am not a military authority on these things."[2] And a little later, Douglas MacArthur, who was a military authority, also threatened to use the atomic bomb. The war continued.

Eisenhower took office early in 1953 and made John Foster Dulles his secretary of state. Ike rescinded Truman's order neutralizing Taiwan. China's leader, Chiang Kai-shek, was now "unleashed." Chiang, it turned out, did not need a leash to keep him on Taiwan. On his pre-election trip to Korea, Eisenhower saw throngs of demonstrators waving signs reading "No Chinese [sic] in Korea." He made no attempt to have Chinese Nationalists reinforce the Eighth Army. U.S. representatives at Panmunjom dropped hints of possible nuclear weapons use, but the Chinese and North Koreans had heard that song before. The war continued, although the Communist forces were becoming increasingly disenchanted with the situation. Offensive after offensive failed to break through the UN line. All the Chinese and North Koreans got were more bodies.

Then something happened in Russia that had a real effect on the war. On March 5, 1953, Josef Stalin died. Ten days later, Georgi Malenkov said that there were disputes between the U.S. and the U.S.S.R. that "cannot be decided by peaceful means, on the basis of mutual understanding."[3] Two weeks later, talks on exchanging POWs began.

The war still went on. On May 25, the Chinese launched a major offensive that continued for two weeks but failed to break through. On June 26, they tried again. Same result.

On July 27, 1953, General William K. Harrison, chief UN negotiator, and General Nam Il, the North Korean chief of state, signed the armistice.

If threats to use nuclear weapons could have ended the war, it would have been over two years earlier. The threat from Truman, which was more credible than that from the Eisenhower administration (Ike also threatened to "unleash" Chiang Kai-shek), didn't change anything, nor did threats from MacArthur. What *did* change things were two bloody repulses of Communist troops and the death of Josef Stalin.

MYTH #27

The Majority of the Troops in Vietnam Were Minorities

There was so much publicity about the number of black troops in the U.S. Army during the Vietnam War that many people believed that the *majority* of the combat troops were members of this minority group.

There was indeed a much larger proportion of African-American troops in Vietnam (at least in combat) than in our previous wars. That is because, during most of our history, the Army would not accept many African Americans. Those they did accept were generally used as truck drivers or unskilled laborers.

In spite of this discrimination, African Americans have played a part in all of America's wars since the Revolution—in some cases, a prominent part. For example, during the British retreat from Concord, General Thomas Gage sent up several wagons loaded with ammunition to help his redcoats. On their way, they were

An African-American soldier training for jungle fighting,
probably in Vietnam. Only a minority of African-American
soldiers had combat duties in either World War, and even
then they were in segregated units. The Army was finally
desegregated during the Korean War, but there was no jungle
fighting in Korea because the peninsula has no jungles.

challenged by a group of older men led by an old black man.
The black man was named David Lamson. He was captain of
an "alarm company" of the local militia. Alarm companies were
composed of men considered too old for most fighting, and
were to be called up only in desperate situations.

The British grenadiers laughed at the old coots and whipped
their horses. Lamson gave a signal and his men shot one horse
in every team, the officer in charge of the British party, and
two sergeants. The grenadiers jumped off the wagons, dropped

their muskets, and ran for their lives. They surrendered to the first person they saw along the road: an old woman tending her garden.

Previously, black militiamen had fought at Lexington and Concord. At Lexington, the very first engagement of the war, a slave named Prince Easterbrooks was one of the minutemen wounded, but that didn't stop him; he went on to serve in almost every major campaign in the Revolution. A fairly large number of African-Americans were among the militia that drove the British out of Concord and harassed them back to Boston, and were also among those who fought on Breeds Hill.

Some were slaves; some were free. Some masters gave their slaves freedom if they would join the fight against the British; some had their slaves join in place of themselves. Some states gave any slave who took part in the war his freedom. Rhode Island purchased a number of slaves, gave them freedom, and created the predominantly black First Rhode Island Regiment.

The Continental Army was established in June 1775. Horatio Gates, its adjutant general, ordered its recruiting officers not to accept "any deserter from the Ministerial army, nor any stroller, negro or vagabond."[1] George Washington, however, countermanded that order and told his officers to continue enlisting free blacks. At the peak of the Revolution, blacks formed approximately 15 percent of the Patriot forces.

In the War of 1812, the Army refused to enlist slaves, but took a few free blacks. The Navy was more liberal, and one sixth of the sailors were black. One crew of blacks even earned the praise of Commodore Oliver Hazard Perry. Before the Battle of New Orleans, Andrew Jackson made a vigorous effort to enlist black soldiers, but in the American armies of that war, only whites could be officers. Both during and after the

War of 1812, the Navy continued to be more open to African-American recruits than the Army. But Isaac Chauncey, acting assistant secretary of the Navy in 1836, sent word to the naval hierarchy "not to enter a greater proportion of colored persons than 5 percent of the whole number of white persons entered."[2]

Blacks were definitely excluded from the Army when the Civil War began, although they were still accepted by the Navy. When Congress passed the Militia Act of 1862, recruitment of blacks again became legal. Enlisting fugitive slaves was not allowed, however. Major General David Hunter, however, charged with occupying the coast of South Carolina, Georgia, and Florida, and denied reinforcements, did just that, but Washington gave him no money to pay or equip his troops. Simon Cameron, the Secretary of War, maintained that the nation had a duty to enlist fugitive slaves. Lincoln fired him and replaced him with Edwin Stanton. Lincoln was afraid that arming fugitive slaves would turn the slave-holding border states, still loyal to the union, into rebels.

Lincoln gradually became convinced that freeing the slaves in the Confederate states would be more advantageous to the Union than the support of some border states, so on January 1, 1863, he issued the Emancipation Proclamation. The black presence in the army rapidly increased until there were 166 mostly black regiments (a majority of the officers in these outfits were white) in the Army. There were 186,000 African Americans among the 2,100,000 men in the Army and another 30,000 in the Navy. Black privates in the Civil War were paid $10 a month from which $3 could be deducted for clothing. White privates got $13 a month with no clothing deduction.

After the Civil War, the military again began to restrict blacks. Ulysses S. Grant said he did not object to black soldiers but thought they should be enlisted in the reserves and called up only in emergencies. In 1866, Congress authorized two cavalry regiments and four infantry regiments to be composed of black enlisted men and mostly white officers. Three years later, it cut the infantry regiments to two: the 24th and the 25th. These were the famous "Buffalo Soldiers" who served mostly on the western frontier. African-American officers were few and far between. A white officer referred to Henry O. Flipper, the first black to graduate from West Point, as "our Ethiopian lieutenant," leading 60 of "the very best darkies who ever stole a chicken."[3]

In the Spanish-American War, Buffalo Soldiers saved Teddy Roosevelt's "Rough Riders" at Las Guasimas and captured the Spanish blockhouse on San Juan Hill, but after the war, Roosevelt belittled the soldiers and gave their white officers all the credit for their accomplishments, forgetting that when the charge up San Juan Hill began, most of those white officers were out of action.

Two segregated black divisions served in World War I: the 92nd and 93rd Infantry Divisions. General John J. Pershing, who had led a black unit in the Spanish American War, distanced himself from the African Americans in this war. He broke up the 93rd and offered the pieces to the French Army, which was delighted with the performance of the black Americans. The 92nd saw little combat under Pershing. Of the 404,308 African-American soldiers in World War I, only 42,000 served in combat units. In spite of all evidence to the contrary, the Army brass at the time was convinced that black soldiers couldn't fight.

World War II began to break down the military's Jim Crow tradition, but among too many of the brass the idea persisted that blacks can't fight. Yet the Navy accepted black sailors for all jobs (not just mess attendants), the Air Force allowed blacks to become pilots, and the Marine Corps fielded black Marines. At the end of the war, the Army had 900,000 black soldiers, including 7,000 black officers—up from just five black Army officers in 1941.

But the Army was still segregated by race—there were black infantry units, black artillery units, black armored units, black MP units, and so forth. In 1948, President Harry S. Truman issued an order banning racial segregation in the military, but it was still being practiced until the middle of the Korean War. The Vietnam War was the first in which there was no barrier to black troops serving in combat unit.

That was such a notable change that it gave rise to the myth that the *majority* of combat troops were black. They actually constituted a little more than the proportion of black people in the country as a whole. In the United States, young men of military age (of all races) made up 14 percent of the population. In Vietnam, black soldiers were about 23 percent. Of course, 23 percent is more than 14 percent, but it is far from a majority.

MYTH #28

There Were Two Attacks on American Ships in the Gulf of Tonkin

Like the Korean War, the Vietnam War was a surreal struggle. In Korea, the United States and its allies fought thousands of Chinese troops, but remained at peace with China. In Vietnam, the enemy was North Vietnam, but we were not at war with North Vietnam for some time. What changed that situation was an attack on two U.S. destroyers by what became known as the Tonkin Gulf ghosts.

The United States' involvement in Vietnam began in 1954 at the end of the war between France and the rebel forces of Ho Chi Minh. The United States supported the newly created state of South Vietnam and later sent military advisers to help South Vietnam's president, Ngo Dinh Diem, who was trying to cope with Communist rebels (nicknamed Viet Cong). In 1961, there were 600 U.S. advisers in South Vietnam. The military problem was more difficult than expected, and the number of advisers grew. By 1963, there were 16,000 advisers.

In addition to sending military advisers to Vietnam, the United States was conducting an intelligence operation code-named DESOTO. American ships cruised in international waters off the coasts of the Soviet Union and China to monitor radio communications. To put pressure on North Vietnam, which had been aiding the Viet Cong, the United States extended DESOTO to North Vietnam and began supporting South Vietnamese commando operations across the demilitarized zone.

On August 2, 1964, the U.S.S. *Maddox*, a destroyer, was conducting a DESOTO patrol when three Vietnamese torpedo boats attacked it. Not reported at the time was the fact that the destroyer's radar crew had reported that the three boats were approaching, and Captain John J. Herrick ordered his gun crews to fire if the torpedo boats got closer than 10,000 yards. So the North Vietnamese did not fire first.

The *Maddox* was well outside the territorial waters claimed by North Vietnam, but the North Vietnamese seemed to think it was aiding the South Vietnamese commandos. Shortly before the attack, South Vietnamese had raided two North Vietnamese islands and mercenary Thai pilots, hired by the CIA, had bombed North Vietnamese border outposts. Four years later, Robert McNamara, U.S. secretary of defense, admitted that U.S. ships *had* been helping the South Vietnamese raiders, although the *Maddox* was not one of them. At any rate, the attack was a rather stupid decision on the part of the North Vietnamese.

The torpedo boats allegedly fired two torpedoes, but both missed. On of them also fired on *Maddox* with a heavy machine gun, which merely compounded the stupidity. No sensible sailor attacks a destroyer with a machine gun. The *Maddox* responded with a shower of shells from its five-inch and three-inch guns, and U.S. carrier planes strafed the North Vietnamese boats. One may have been sunk, one caught fire, and one was less heavily damaged.

Two days later, the *Maddox* again went on DESOTO patrol, this time joined by another destroyer, the U.S.S. *C. Turner Joy.* The weather was stormy, and U.S. radar and sonar operators reported hostile naval craft and torpedoes. Both destroyers opened fire on targets appearing on their radar screens but unseen from the ships. Captain Herrick reported the attack, but later expressed doubt that any attack had occurred.

President Lyndon B. Johnson expressed no doubt when he told Congress about the attack on August 5.

> Last night, I announced to the American people that the North Vietnamese had conducted further deliberate attacks against U.S. naval vessels operating in international waters, and I had therefore directed air action against the gunboats and supporting facilities used in these hostile operations.... After consultation with the leaders of both parties in Congress, I further announced a decision to ask the Congress for a resolution expressing the unity and determination of the United States in supporting freedom and in protecting peace in southeast Asia.
>
> These latest actions of the North Vietnamese regime has given a new and grave turn to the already serious situation in southeast Asia.... This is not just a jungle war, but a struggle for freedom on every front of human activity. Our military and economic assistance to South Vietnam and Laos in particular has the purpose of helping these countries to repel aggression and strengthen their independence.

As President of the United States, I have concluded that I should now ask Congress, on its part, to join in affirming the national determination that all such attacks will be met, and that the United States will continue its basic policy of assisting the free nations of the area to defend their freedom.[1]

President Lyndon B. Johnson used the report of a North Korean attack on U.S. Naval ships to get Congress to agree to stepping up the war in Vietnam. The trouble was that the Tonkin Gulf attack never happened.

Congress passed a joint resolution stating that "Congress approves and supports the determination of the President to take all necessary measures to repel any armed attack against the forces of the United States and to repel any further aggression."[2]

That was as close to a declaration of war against North Vietnam as was ever made. It led to a huge increase in troop strength in Vietnam and the bombing of North Vietnamese cities. U.S. troops would no longer be mere advisers; they would be combat troops. North Vietnamese troops would no longer merely smuggle supplies to the Viet Cong; they would cross the border to fight. And a lot of people on both sides would die.

On December 1, 2005, the National Security Agency declassified 140 Top Secret documents showing not only that there was no second attack in the Tonkin Gulf but that the report of one was a deliberate prevarication. The targets the U.S. ships fired at that night have become known as the "ghosts of Tonkin Gulf." What followed was our only war to have been provoked by ghosts.

MYTH #29

Khe Sanh Survived a Terrible Siege

1968 was the Year of the Monkey in the Calendar of the Twelve Beasts, the Chinese Zodiac that was followed in China, Korea, Vietnam, and other parts of the Far East. As the new year approached, General Vo Nguyen Giap, minister of war in North Vietnam, may have been thinking of the monkey hunters of southeast Asia, who captured monkeys to be sold to zoos or pet stores. One of their techniques, according to a widely held belief, was to drill a hole in a large coconut and put a bright bead in the hole. After a while, a curious monkey would see the bead and reach into the hole to get it. After the monkey closed his fist on the bead, he found he could not take his hand out of the hole. But monkeys are stubborn as well as curious, so the monkey wouldn't let go of the bead. A small monkey attached to a large coconut can't move very fast, so he usually ended up in a cage.

The shiny bead General Giap planned to use was a place called Khe Sanh, near the border between North and South Vietnam, where the U.S. Marines had a base. The coconut was the North Vietnamese army. And the monkey was General William C. Westmoreland, the U.S. commander in Vietnam.

General William Westmoreland (in civilian dress) and General Paul Harkins as Westmoreland takes over in Vietnam. Westmoreland's fascination with Khe Sahn paved the way for the Tet Offensive.

There had been a considerable amount of fighting in the hills near the border between the two Vietnams. On January 17, 1968, a Marine patrol from Khe Sanh was ambushed. There were more skirmishes with patrols from Khe Sanh on January 19 and 20. Aerial reconnaissance showed that the North Vietnamese had cut two new roads through the jungle from Laos that gave access to trails leading to Khe Sanh. Aerial observers saw trenches snaking out of the jungle and surrounding the barbed wire perimeter of Khe Sanh. North Vietnamese shells began falling on the base.

Westmoreland's headquarters told the press that the largest battle of the war was shaping up at Khe Sanh. Giap was supposed to have 20,000 North Vietnam Army (NVA) troops in the vicinity of Khe Sanh. There were 6,000 Marines inside the fortified base. Briefing officers told reporters there were 40,000 more troops close by. According to Michael Herr in *Esquire,* the number was more like a quarter of a million.[1]

A large battle was what Westmoreland was anxiously waiting for. NVA troops hiding in the woods like guerrillas and Viet Cong living in their villages disguised as simple farmers were not war—at least not the kind of war "Westy" and his men had trained for. It looked to Westmoreland that Giap, the conqueror of Dien Bien Phu, was planning to make Khe Sanh another Dien Bien Phu. Like Dien Bien Phu, Khe Sanh was a fortified base in the jungle, largely air supplied. But Giap's tactics at the French base would not work at Khe Sanh. U.S. air power was immensely more powerful than was that of the French. The United States had far more troops in the area, and the NVA firepower could not even compare with that of the Americans.

A North Vietnamese lieutenant waving a white flag confirmed Westmoreland's hopes. He said he had served in the NVA faithfully for 14 years, but his superiors had ignored his service and his qualifications and promoted a less qualified officer. So he was surrendering. The Americans interrogated him. His information about North Vietnamese positions jibed so well with what the U.S. forces knew that they had to believe him. He said an attack on Khe Sanh with an overwhelming force would take place the next day, at 12:39 a.m.

If anyone doubted that a soldier who had fought for his cause for 14 years would surrender because of a missed promotion, those doubts ended at 12:30 a.m. A hurricane of artillery shells, mortar shells, and rockets landed on the base. NVA troops pushed Bangalore torpedoes under the barbed wire and blasted pathways through it. One rocket hit an ammunition bunker, and 15 tons of explosives went off at once, flattening tents and toppling helicopters. To repel rats, the Marines had soaked the sandbags of their bunkers in fuel oil. The explosion set fire to the bunkers. A shell struck a second ammunition dump and another thousand pounds of explosives disappeared in an enormous blast. The two explosions destroyed 98 percent of the Marines' ammunition, but they held on. Marine aircraft strafed the jungle, and artillery from the supporting bases pounded suspected NVA artillery positions, but the North Vietnamese were expert at camouflaging everything and at hiding their artillery in caves and deep emplacements immune to everything but a direct hit.

The odd thing about the attack was that the North Vietnamese must have known that the American base was in bad shape after the ammo dumps blew up, but they didn't press the attack. Instead of the "human sea" the Marines were expecting, they estimated that there were only about a thousand attackers.

Westmoreland decided that the attack was merely a probe to test American strength at Khe Sanh. He ordered his forces to be ready to implement "Plan Niagara."

"Niagara" would take advantage of U.S. air power. Every aircraft in the area—helicopters, fighter bombers, even the giant B-52 strategic bombers—would drown the attackers with bombs, bullets, rockets, and shells.

The weather didn't cooperate.

For days the Khe Sanh area was covered with a pea soup fog that obscured any possible targets for aircraft. The planes dropped bombs, hoping they'd hit something, and the artillery fired into the area around Khe Sanh. The NVA artillery also continued firing, and North Vietnamese regulars continued ambushing patrols based on Khe Sanh. Whenever the fog cleared, aerial observers saw that the network of approach trenches around Khe Sanh was becoming ever more elaborate.

Officers at Westmoreland's headquarters knew that North Vietnam's big push could begin at any moment. Briefing officers told reporters that Khe Sanh was surrounded, but it was vital to hold it because it blocked enemy infiltration routes. They didn't explain how it blocked those routes if the enemy was behind the base. General Earle Wheeler, chairman of the Joint Chiefs of Staff, told *Time* that the loss of Khe Sanh would allow the Communists to "roll from the mountains of Laos right down to the South China Sea."[2]

The interesting thing about Wheeler's analysis was that it came *after* Giap had sneaked 84,000 men south through the jungles and hit all of the major cities of South Vietnam in what was called the "Tet Offensive."

Tet is the Vietnamese (and Chinese and Korean) New Year. It is a major holiday, and both sides in the Vietnam War had observed an unofficial cease fire. Many South Vietnamese soldiers were home with their families. The offensive took the U.S. and South Vietnam forces by surprise. North Vietnamese regulars and Viet Cong (South Korean Communist guerrillas) sneaked into the cities disguised as civilians and smuggled in rocket launchers, machine guns, mortars, and rifles.

They struck while Westmoreland was still holding tightly to Khe Sanh with his enormous military fist. "Westy" believed the Tet Offensive was a diversion instead of the main show.

American troops were still concentrated in the north and watching the Khe Sanh area while Giap's legions were laying waste to the south. Fortunately, their intelligence was faulty and their tactics were worse—they used companies to attack targets that called for at least a battalion. The Communist troops were eventually driven out of all the southern cities with enormous loss of life.

The Tet Offensive was long gone, but the "siege" of Khe Sanh continued. American bombers dropped an enormous tonnage of bombs on the area around Khe Sanh, including armor-piercing bombs intended to penetrate the tunnels U.S. intelligence believed the NVA were digging.

But bombardment of Khe Sanh dropped off. There were fewer signs of enemy activity near the base. Further, the Tet Offensive had shown how utterly useless Khe Sanh was to the security of South Vietnam. At length, just about everyone but Westmoreland concluded that Vo Nguyen Giap had pulled off one of the biggest military deceptions since the Trojan Horse.

But the "impending battle" had received so much publicity, the base could not merely be abandoned. It had to be liberated. That job fell to the 1st Air Cavalry, troopers who rode to battle in helicopters instead of on horses.

As correspondent Robert Pisor put it, "The commander of the 1st Air Cav, Lieutenant General John J. Tolson, knew it was a charade. He had read the intelligence reports and did not expect to find any North Vietnamese at Khe Sanh."[3]

And he didn't. He found few weapons, and few signs that a large force had been in the area. American planes had dropped 90 tons of bombs on the small plateau that had been occupied by the NVA. That's more than had been dropped on all of Europe in 1942 and 1943. The only result was a lot of churned-up dirt. The "tunnel-busting" bombs didn't bust any tunnels, because there were no tunnels. There were trenches, but they looked different on the ground than they did in the air. Douglas Robinson of the *New York Times* described them: "Some of the zigzag trenches come within a few feet of the barbed wire on the edge of the mined no-man's-land that separated the Marines from their attackers by about 30 yards. However, the trenches are only 14 to 20 inches deep and wide enough for just one man at a time to crawl toward the Marine positions."[4]

Westmoreland claimed that Khe Sanh was a great victory for the United States. "We took 200 killed at Khe Sanh and about 800 wounded and evacuated," he said. "The enemy by my count has suffered at least 15,000 dead in this area."[5]

Westmoreland's count depended on a new way of figuring enemy casualties. The traditional body count wouldn't work, because when Khe Sanh was relieved, there were few bodies to count. So "Westy" relied on the computers of his Systems Analysis Office. The official Air Force history of the Khe Sanh operations explained: "General Westmoreland's Systems Analysis Office prepared four mathematical models from which its technicians concluded that the total enemy killed and wounded numbered between 49 and 65 percent of the force that began the siege—between 9,800 and 13,000 men. The generally cited estimate, 10,000, is half the number of North Vietnamese troops believed committed at the outset of the operation."[6]

This does require a couple of unprovable assumptions: (1) that there were 20,000 enemy troops around Khe Sanh in the first place, and (2) that they were there after the Tet Offensive began. The first is possible. The second is highly improbable, especially as some of the NVA units known to have been in the

vicinity of Khe Sanh early in the operation have been identified as being among those taking part in the Tet Offensive in
southern South Vietnam.

What appears certain is that for most of the time it was
"under siege," Khe Sanh was besieged by ghosts.

Notes

Chapter 1

1. Parker, *Cambridge Illustrated History*, p. 2.
2. Ibid., p. 5.
3. Ibid.
4. Rodgers, *Greek and Roman*, pp. 15–16.
5. Weir, *50 Military Leaders*, pp. 27–28.
6. Parker, p. 5.
7. Parker, p. 9.
8. Parker, p. 3.

Chapter 2

1. See Chadwick, *Mycenaean World*, pp. 164–72.
2. Snodgrass, *Arms and Armor*, p. 17.
3. Pope, Saxton T. *Bows and Arrows*, p. 56.

Chapter 3

1. Some writers say the White Huns were a Caucasian race. This is as silly as maintaining that the Blue Turks were Martians (blue is the color of the east). The use of colors to indicate directions originated with the Chinese, who also used black for the north,

red for the south, and yellow or gold for the center. This symbolism was adopted by the Central Asian nomads, hence the Golden Horde for the central kingdom of the Mongol empire and the Red Sea and Black Sea, respectively the sea south of Turkey and the sea north of Turkey. There were and have been for centuries many Caucasian nomads in Central Asia, such as the Scythians and the Alans, but the Huns were not among them.

2. So, possibly, was Alatheus, the other regent. See Dawson, *Making of Europe*, p. 89.

3. Burns, " Battle of Adrianople," pp. 336–45.

Chapter 4

1. Tarassuk and Blair, *Complete Encyclopedia*, pp. 42–45.

2. Keegan, *Illustrated Face*, pp. 69–93.

Chapter 5

1. Tarassuk and Blair, p. 96.

2. Pope, Saxton T., *Bows and Arrows*, pp. 32–33. "Toxophilus" was the pen name of Roger Ascham, who wrote about archery in the 16th century. "Ishi" was a friend of Dr. Pope, the last surviving member of the Yana Indian tribe of California. He taught Pope the Yana style of archery and made flight arrows.

3. Pope, Saxton T., *Bows and Arrows*, pp. 8–29.

4. Ibid., pp. 27–28.

5. Payne-Gallwey, *Crossbow*, p. 21.

6. The crossbow's rate of fire is often give as one shot a minute. But that is the rate for later, far more powerful crossbows,

which were bent with the aid of a windlass and pulleys. The crossbows at Crecy were bent by the crossbowman stooping down, placing a hook attached to his belt on the bowstring, and standing up.

7. Payne-Gallwey, *Crossbow*, p. 27.

8. Ibid., p. 15.

Chapter 6

1. Pope, Dudley, *Guns*, p. 32.

2. McNeill, *Pursuit of Power*, pp. 61, 81, 87.

3. Pope, Dudley, *Guns*, p.38.

Chapter 7

1. Peterson, *Arms and Armor*, p. 307.

2. Ibid., p. 309.

3. Marks, *And Die in the West*, p. 359. Also Cunningham, Eugene. *Triggernometry*. Caldwell, Idaho: Caxton Printers, p. 123.

Chapter 8

1. Davis, *Great Battles*, p. 20.

2. Perrin, *Giving up the Gun*, p. 25.

3. Korean Spirit and Culture, *Admiral Yi Sun-sin*, pp. 34–38.

4. Ibid., p. 60.

5. Conlon, *Weapons and Fighting*, p.192.

6. Ballard, George Alexander, *The Influence of the Sea on the Political History of Japan*, p. 57. Quoted in Korean Spirit and Culture, *Admiral Yi Sun-sin*, p. 23.

Chapter 9

1. There is some justification for this feeling. General Thomas Gage had spent most of his life in what became the United States and hoped to retire to an estate in New York or New Jersey. His wife was an American. Benjamin Franklin was as celebrated in England as in the colonies and was a prominent member of London high society. There was a strong Tory movement among the small farmers in the South, but, as we'll see, it had nothing to do with loyalty to the crown.

Chapter 10

1. Held, "Kentucky Rifle," p. 358.
2. Peterson, *Arms and Armor*, p. 204.
3. Ibid., p. 163.
4. Ibid., p. 198.
5. Hatcher, *Textbook of Pistols*, p. 148.
6. Held, "Kentucky Rifle," p. 357.
7. Ibid.
8. Peterson, *Arms and Armor*, p. 200.
9. Peterson, *Book of the Continental Soldier*, p. 26.

Chapter 11

1. Peterson, *Arms and Armor*, p. 200.
2. Ketchum, *Saratoga*, p. 126.

Chapter 13

1. Montgomery, "If Ponies Rode Men," *http://americanrevolution. org/upside.html.*

Chapter 14

1. Pratt, *Ordeal*, p.183.
2. Morison, *Oxford History*, p. 615.
3. Size of Union and Confederate Armies, *www.civilwarhome. com/armysize.htm.*
4. Eggenberger, *Encyclopedia of Battles*, p. 19.
5. Ibid., p. 171.
6. Not "fustest with the mostest." Forrest was a pretty rough character, but he was neither uneducated nor a dumbell.
7. Pratt, *Ordeal*, p. 250.
8. Downey, *Storming of the Gateway*, p. 224.
9. Pratt, *Ordeal*, p. 283.

Chapter 15

1. Toland, *Ships in the Sky*, p. 13.
2. Ibid., p. 14.
3. Ibid., p. 15
4. Ibid., p. 16.
5. Ibid., p.17
6. Ibid.
7. Ibid.
8. Toland, *Ships in the Sky*, p. 18.
9. Ibid.
10. Toland, *Ships in the Sky*, p. 19.

Chapter 16

1. Connell, *Son of the Morning Star*, pp. 257–8.

Chapter 17

1. Crow, *Epic of Latin America*, p. 607. Population figures from this period are hazy. They are extrapolated from an inaccurate census taken a generation earlier. But the tremendous loss of life was quite obvious.

2. "War of the Triple Alliance," *http://countrystudies.us/paraguay /11.htm.*

3. "Wars of the World," *www.onwar.com/aced/data/tango/ triple1864.htm.* As mentioned earlier, these figures can only be approximations.

4. Crow, *Epic*, p.607.

Chapter 18

1. O'Toole, *Spanish War*, p. 386.

2. *Moro* means "Moor" in Spanish. When the Spanish first met the Moros in the 16th century, the only Muslims they were familiar with were Moors.

3. Bain, *Sitting in Darkness*, p.77.

4. Ibid., pp. 184–85. Also, O'Toole, *Spanish War*, p. 388.

5. Bain, *Sitting in Darkness*, p. 185.

6. Single-action revolvers, like those of movie cowboys, are fired by pulling back the hammer and squeezing the trigger. Double-action revolvers may be fired by a long pull on the trigger, although most of them may also be fired the same way as the single-actions.

7. "Battle of Bud Bagsak," Wikipedia.

Chapter 19

1. Coe et al., *Swords*, p. 82.
2. Reid, *Weapons*, p. 230.
3. Ibid.
4. Coe et al. p.124. Also, Chivers, *The Gun*, p. 124.
5. Chivers, *The Gun*, p. 110.

Chapter 20

1. Liddell Hart, *History*, p 19.
2. Halle, *Tanks*, p.128.
3. Keegan, John, *Second World War*, pp.59–60.
4. Morris et al., *Weapons*, pp. 141–42.
5. Horne, *To Lose a Battle*, p. 182.
6. Taylor, *Second World War*, p. 49.

Chapter 22

1. Fuller, *Reader's Companion*, quoted in Weir, *50 Military Leaders*, p. 196.
2. Weir, *50 Military Leaders*, p. 197.
3. Liddell Hart, *History*, p. 595.
4. Taylor, *Second World War*, p. 179.
5. Liddell Hart, *History*, p. 612.

Chapter 23

1. Taylor, *Second World War*, p.168.
2. Keegan and Wheatcroft, *Who's Who*, p. 201.
3. Ibid.

4. Bain, *Sitting in Darkness*, p. 210.

5. Manchester, *American Caesar*, p. 43.

6. Ibid., p. 52.

7. Mason, *Great Pursuit*, p. 43.

8. Full disclosure: one of the sailors in that occupying force was my father, Luke S. Weir. Incidentally, the weapons reached Huerta through another port.

9. Keith, *Sixguns*.

10. James, D. Clayton. *The Years of MacArthur*, vol. I, 1880-1941. Boston: Houghton Mifflin, 1970, p. 125.

11. They also got M-1917 rifles, which have been described as "obsolete" and "decrepit." They were neither. Many people, including Maj. Gen. Julian Hatcher of the U.S. Army Ordnance Dept., considered the M-1917 a better rifle than the beloved M-1903 Springfield, which many U.S. troops were carrying until 1943. The M-1917, nicknamed the Enfield because it was developed at that arsenal in England, was at least as good as any rifle in the hands of any foreign soldiers in the world during World War II.

12. "MacArthur deserts 'The Battling Bastards of Bataan.'"

13. Kim's parents were refugees from Japanese rule living in the Soviet Union.

14. Alexander, *Korea*, p. 148.

15. Ridgway, *Korean War*, p. 42.

16. Alexander, *Korea*, p. 368.

17. Ibid., p. 372.

18. Ibid., p. 384.

19. Ibid., pp. 405–06.

20. Ibid., pp. 406–07.

Chapter 24

1. Astor, *Right to Fight*, p. 320.
2. Ibid.
3. Astor, *Right to Fight*, p. 321.
4. Ibid., p. 316.

Chapter 25

1. Weir, "Public Information," p.210. Also Blair, *Forgotten War*, p. 975.

Chapter 26

1. Blair, *Forgotten War*, pp. 522–23. Also Alexander, *Korea*, p.371.
2. Blair, *Forgotten War*, p. 523.
3. Ibid., p. 971.

Chapter 27

1. Quarles, *Negro*, p. 15.
2. Astor, *Right to Fight*, p. 19.
3. Ibid., p. 46.

Chapter 28

1. Fuller, *Reader's Companion*.
2. Ibid.

Chapter 29

1. Herr, Dispatches, p. 107.

2. *Time*, March 1, 1968.

3. Pisor, *End of the Line*, p. 218.

4. *New York Times*, April 10, 1968.

5. *Time*, April 12, 1968, p. 30

6. Nalty, *Air Power*, p. 103.

Bibliography

Alexander, Bevin. *Korea: The First War We Lost.* New York: Hippocrene Books, 1998.

Astor, Gerald. *The Right to Fight.* Cambridge, Mass.: Da Capo Press, 2001.

Bain, David Haward. *Sitting in Darkness: America in the Philippines.* Boston: Houghton Mifflin, 1984.

"Battle of Bud Bagsak." Wikipedia. *http://en.wikipilipinas. org/index.php?title=Battle_of_Bud_Bagsak* (accessed June 2011).

Blair, Clay. *The Forgotten War: America in Korea, 1950–1953.* New York: Times Books, 1987.

Burns, T.S. "The Battle of Adrianople: A Reconsideration." *Historia* xxii, DATE OF PUB.

Chadwick, John. *The Mycenaean World.* Cambridge, England: The Cambridge University Press, 1976.

Chivers, C.J. *The Gun.* New York: Simon & Schuster, 2010.

Coe, Michael D., Peter Connolly, Anthony Harding, Victor Harris, Donald J. LaRocca, Anthony North, Thom Richardson, Christopher Spring, and Frederick Wilkinson. *Swords and Hilt Weapons.* New York: Barnes & Noble, 1993.

Conlon, Thomas D. *Weapons and Fighting Techniques of the Samurai Warrior*. New York: Metro Books, 2008.

Connell, Evan S. *Son of the Morning Star*. San Francisco: North Point Press, 1984.

Crow, John A. *The Epic of Latin America, 4th Edition*. Berkeley, Calif.: University of California Press, 1952.

Davis, William C., ed. *Great Battles of the Civil War*. New York: Beekman House (n.d.).

Dawson, Christopher. *The Making of Europe*. New York: Meridian Books, 1959.

Downey, Fairfax. *Storming of the Gateway*. New York: David Mckay, 1960.

Eggenberger, David. *An Encyclopedia of Battles*. New York: Dover Publications, 1967.

Fuller, J.F.C. *The Reader's Companion to Military History, Gulf of Tonkin*. On "The Avalon Project" Website for Yale Law School, "The Tonkin Gulf Incident; 1964." *http://avalon.law.yale.edu/20th_century/tonkin-g.asp* (accessed June 2011).

Halle, Armin. *Tanks: An Illustrated History of Fighting Vehicles*. Greenwich, Conn.: New York Graphic Society, 1971.

Hatcher, J.S.

Held, Robert. "The Kentucky Rifle—Fact and Fiction" in *Gun Digest Treasury*. Chicago: Gun Digest Company, 1966.

Herr, Michael. *Dispatches*. New York: Knopf, 1977.

Horne, Alistair. *To Lose a Battle: France 1940*. Boston: Little, Brown, 1969.

James, D. Clayton. *The Years of MacArthur, Vol. I, 1880–1941*. Boston: Houghton Mifflin, 1970.

Keegan, John. *The Illustrated Face of Battle*. New York: Viking Penguin, 1989.

———. *The Second World War*. New York: Penguin, 1990.

Keegan, John, and Andrew Wheatcroft. *Who's who in Military History*. New York: William Morrow, 1976.

Keith, Elmer. *Sixguns by Keith, 1961 Revised Edition*. Livonia, N.Y.: RR Books, 1961.

Ketchum, Richard M. *Saratoga: Turning Point in America's Revolutionary War*. London: Pimlico, 1999.

Korean Spirit and Culture. *Admiral Yi Sun-sin: A Brief Overview of His Life and Achievement*. Seoul (n.d.).

Liddell Hart, B.H. *History of the Second World War*. New York: Putnam's, 1971.

"MacArthur deserts 'The Battling Bastards of Bataan' and escapes to Australia." *www.pacificwar.org.au/Philippines/Macescapes.html* (accessed June 2011).

Manchester, William. *American Caesar: Douglas MacArthur, 1880–1964*. New York: Dell, 1979.

Marks, Paula Mitchell. *And Die in the West*. New York: Simon and Schuster, 1989.

Mason, Herbert Molloy, Jr. *The Great Pursuit*. New York: Random House, 1970.

Mayor, Adrienne. *Greek Fire, Poison Arrows and Scorpion Bombs*. Woodstock, N.Y.: Overlook Duckworth, 2003.

McNeill, William H. *The Pursuit of Power*. Chicago: University of Chicago Press, 1982.

Montgomery, Dennis. "If Ponies Rode Men and Grass Ate the Cows." American Revolution.org. *http://americanrevolution.org/upside.html* (accessed June 2011).

Morison, Samuel Eliot. *The Oxford History of the American People*. New York: Oxford University Press, 1965.

Morris, Eric, Curt Johnson, Christopher Chant, and H.P. Willmott. *Weapons and Warfare of the Twentieth Century.* Secaucus, N.J.: Derbibooks, 1976.

Nalty, Bernard C. *Air Power and the Fight for Khe Sanh.* Washington, D.C.: Office of Air Force History, U.S. Air Force, 1973.

O'Toole, G.J.A. *The Spanish War: An American Epic, 1898.* New York: W.W. Norton, 1984.

Parker, Geoffrey, ed. *The Cambridge Illustrated History of Warfare: The Triumph of the West.* Cambridge, England: The Cambridge University Press, 1995.

Payne-Gallwey, Ralph. *The Crossbow.* London: The Holland Press, 1986.

Perrin, Noel. *Giving Up the Gun: Japan's Reversion to the Sword.* Boston: David Godine, 1979.

Peterson, Harold L. *Arms and Armor in Colonial America, 1526–1783.* New York, Bramhall House, 1956.

————. The Book of the Continental Soldier. Pittsburgh: Stackpole, 1968.

Pisor, Robert. *The End of the Line: The Siege of Khe Sanh.* New York: Ballentine, 1985.

Pope, Dudley. *Guns.* Feltham, Middlesex, England: Hamlyn House, 1970.

Pope, Saxton T. *Bows and Arrows.* Berkeley, Calif.: University of California Press, 1962.

Pratt, Fletcher. *Ordeal by Fire.* New York: William Sloan Associates, 1948, and New York: Dover Publications, 1997.

Quarles, Benjamin. *The Negro in the American Revolution.* Chapel Hill, N.C.: University of North Carolina Press, 1996.

Reid, William. *Weapons Through the Ages*. New York: Crescent Books, 1986.

Ridgway, Matthew B. *The Korean War: How We Met the Challenge; How All-Out Asian War was Averted; Why MacArthur Was Dismissed; Why Today's War Objectives Must Be Limited*. Garden City, N.Y.: Doubleday, 1967.

Robinson, Douglas. *New York Times*, April 10, 1968.

Rodgers, William Ledyard. *Greek and Roman Naval Warfare*. Annapolis, Md.: U.S. Naval Institute, 1964.

"Size of the Union and Confederate Armies." *www.civilwarhome. com/armysize.htm* (accessed June 2011).

Snodgrass, A.M. *Arms and Armor of the Greeks*. Ithaca, N.Y.: Cornell University Press, 1967.

Tarassuk, Leonid, and Claude Blair. *The Complete Encyclopedia of Arms and Weapons*. New York: Bonanza Books, 1986.

Taylor, A.J.P. *The Second World War*. New York: Putnam's, 1975.

Time magazine, March 1, 1968.

Time magazie, April 12, 1968.

Toland, John. *Ships in the Sky*. New York: Henry Holt, 1957.

"The War of the Triple Alliance." *http://countrystudies.us/paraguay /11.htm* (accessed June 2011).

"*War of the Triple Alliance 1864–1870.*" *OnWar.com*. *www. onwar.com/aced/data/tango/triple1864.htm* (accessed June 2011).

Weir, William. *50 Military Leaders Who Changed the World*. Franklin Lakes, N.J.: Career Press, 2007.

———. "Public Information." *War, Literature and the Arts* 10, No. 1 (Spring–Summer 1998).

INDEX

About the Author

William Weir has been a newspaper reporter, a military policeman, an Army combat correspondent in the Korean War, a public relations specialist for a large telephone company, and a freelance magazine writer specializing in crime and military subjects. He has written some 50 articles for publications ranging from the *New York Times* to *Connecticut Magazine*. He has written 12 previous books:

Written With Lead:
Legendary American Gunfights and Gunfighters (1992)

Fatal Victories (1993)

In the Shadow of the Dope Fiend:
America's War on Drugs (1995)

A Well Regulated Militia:
The Battle Over Gun Control (1997)

50 Battles That Changed the World (2001)

Soldiers in the Shadows: Unknown Warriors Who
Changed the Course of History (2002)

The Encyclopedia of African American Military History
(2004)

50 Weapons That Changed Warfare (2005)

Turning Points in Military History (2005)

Guerrilla Warfare (2008)

History's Greatest Lies (2009)

Border Patrol (2010)

Three of the books have been reprinted in paperback (*Fatal Victories* twice) and three in hardcover. *50 Battles* has been published in Portuguese, Czech, Polish, Korean, and Chinese. *50 Weapons* has also been published in Czech, and *Turning Points* will be published in Polish. It, like *Fatal Victories*, will also be sold by the Military Book Club.

Weir and his wife, Anne, live in Connecticut and take pride in the achievements of their three adult children.